Presented by
Mr. & Mrs. Perry Euchner
in memory of
Mrs. Louise Doty Colt

D1566760

/\\/\\/\\/\\/\\

Man vs. The Welfare State

/\\/\\/\\/\\/\\
.\\.\\.\\.\\.\\.\\

MAN

VS.

THE

WELFARE

STATE

/\\/\\/\\/\\/\\
.\\.\\.\\.\\.\\.\\

HENRY HAZLITT

ARLINGTON HOUSE   NEW ROCHELLE, N.Y.

Library of Congress Catalog Card Number 72-93457

SBN 87000-066-7

MANUFACTURED IN THE UNITED STATES OF AMERICA

Preface

THIS BOOK GREW OUT OF A PAMPHLET THAT APPEARED IN August, 1968, called *Life and Death of the Welfare State.* The greater part of the material in it is new, but several chapters have appeared in advance of this publication in *The Freeman* (a monthly published by the Foundation for Economic Education at Irvington-on-Hudson, New York), parts of several chapters appeared in my syndicated newspaper column for the Los Angeles Times Syndicate, and Chapter 16 was published as a pamphlet in Europe in English, French, and German editions by INFRA (The International Freedom Academy). I am grateful to the publishers concerned for permission to republish this material here.

HENRY HAZLITT

Wilton, Conn.
August, 1969

/\/\/\/\/\

Contents

/\/\/\/\/\

Man vs. The Welfare State

/\\/\\/\\/\\/\\

CHAPTER 1

Instant Utopia

IN AMERICA TODAY MOST OF THE OLDER GENERA-
tion—and many of the young—stand appalled at the
nihilism of the self-styled Now Generation and its demands for unattainable reforms, or merely for the sheer
destruction of whatever is established.

But the cynicism, nihilism, and revolt of "youth," and
even of some of its parents, are the result of a common
cause. In the last generation politicians and governments have been promising the voters that they could
not only bring perpetual full employment, prosperity,
and "economic growth," but solve the age-old problem
of poverty overnight. And the end result is not merely
that accomplishment has fallen far short of promises,
but that the attempt to fulfill the promises has brought

an enormous increase in government spending, an
enormous increase in the burden of taxes, chronic deficits, chronic inflation, and a constant loss in the buying
power of the people's earnings and savings. "Social
Security" has brought an ominous increase in social in-
security.

Another result of the promise of instant utopia has
been a gigantic growth of governmental power—of in-
terference in the details of everybody's business and
everybody's life. As this power has increased, it has also
become concentrated in fewer and fewer hands. In
America the towns and villages have steadily lost power
to the States, the States to the Federal Government, and
Congress to the President.

One mark of the welfare state everywhere has been
the gathering of power into the hands of one man. This
is no mere unfortunate coincidence; it has been inevitable. Thirty-six years ago the eminent Swedish economist Gustav Cassel explained in a prophetic lecture
how "planned economy," long enough continued, must
lead to despotism:

> The leadership of the State in economic affairs which advo-
> cates of Planned Economy want to establish is, as we have
> seen, necessarily connected with a bewildering mass of gov-
> ernment interferences of a steadily cumulative nature. The
> arbitrariness, the mistakes and the inevitable contradictions
> of such policy will, as daily experience shows, only
> strengthen the demand for a more rational coordination of
> the different measures and, therefore, for unified leadership.
> For this reason Planned Economy will always develop into
> Dictatorship.

The succeeding chapters of this book explain in detail the ideology and methods behind the present inflation and aggrandizement of State power, the conditions

to which it has led and, finally, the solutions we must apply if this sinister threat—not only to the economic future of the American people but to the future of civilization itself—is to be averted.

/\.\/\.\/\.\/\.\

CHAPTER 2

Salvation Through Government Spending

/\.\/\.\/\.\/\.\/\.\/\.\/\.\/\.\/\.\/\.\/\.\/\.\/\.\/\.\/\.\/\.\/\.\

IN THE EARLY NINETEEN THIRTIES, IN THE DEPTH OF the Great Depression, the theory became fashionable that the cause of all depressions was Lack of Purchasing Power. The people just did not have enough money, and because of unwarranted pessimism they were refusing to spend enough even of what they had. The solution was therefore simple: at such a time the government should boldly increase its own spending, "prime the pump," and "get things moving again."

Naive advocates of this theory assumed that more government spending was the whole answer. The more sophisticated advocates saw that the increased spending would not give people more purchasing power if the government kept the budget balanced and took it all away again in higher taxes. The thing to do was to spend more *without* taxing more. The trick, in other words, was deliberately to unbalance the budget—to run a deficit.

Most of the champions of deficits—including the eminent John Maynard Keynes himself, the theory's chief architect—at least publicly professed to believe that the required deficit could be financed by selling bonds directly to the public, to be paid for out of savings. But again, the more sophisticated deficiteers must have seen that a man who buys a $1,000 bond out of his savings surrenders that much purchasing power for the life of the bond. In short, he loses just as much buying power as the government gains. On net balance, no new buying power has been created.

How, then, can the government "create" new purchasing power? It can do so only if it does not increase taxes at all, but "sells" its bonds to the banking system, and if the banks "pay" for them by creating deposit credits on their books in favor of the government. This leads to an increase in "the money supply"—that is, an increase either in the amount of currency or of demand bank deposits.

If the government's new bonds are sold directly to member banks, there tends to be a dollar-for-dollar increase in the money supply compared with the amount of new bonds. But if the government's securities get into the hands of the Federal Reserve Banks, they are used to create what is called "high-powered" money. This can lead to the creation of about $6 of new money for every dollar of new government securities.

It is not easy to give a satisfactory but short explanation of the reason for this to readers without any previous knowledge of monetary theory. When member banks "buy" government bonds and "pay" for them by creating a deposit credit on their books against which the government can draw, they are adding to the nation's supply of purchasing media. They are creating money out of government promises, and some would say they are creating money out of thin air.

Now if a member bank that has bought such government bonds sells them to its regional Federal Reserve Bank, it can ask that Reserve bank to credit the proceeds to the member bank's reserves with that Reserve bank. But if the member bank is a "city bank," it is required to keep a reserve with the Federal Reserve Bank of only 16½ per cent against its net demand deposits. This means that the member bank is entitled to lend, and so create demand deposits for, about six times the amount of its reserves with the Federal Reserve Bank. That is why money created directly or indirectly by the Federal Reserve Banks is called "high-powered" money.

Thus new "purchasing power" is brought into being. Thus people have more money to buy more goods, create more jobs, stimulate more output, and restore prosperity.

At least so it seems for the moment. But soon there are other consequences.

If there have been heavy unemployment and much "idle capacity," the new monetary purchasing power in the system, by increasing the demand for commodities, may indeed lead to an increase in production, and hence to an increase in employment. This has been hailed as the great Keynesian contribution to economic theory and policy. But there are fatal flaws in it.

Unless there were some serious lack of coordination among prices, costs, and wages, mass unemployment would not exist in the first place. When it does exist, the only appropriate cure is individual adjustment of prices, costs, and wages to each other—the return of coordination. But this can be brought about automatically only if the competitive forces of the market are given free play.

The reason the Keynesian medicine can work—under special conditions and for short periods—is that by increasing monetary demand and prices it may increase both sales and profit margins, and so restore production and employment. Yet this could be done even more effectively—and without the poisonous side-effects and after-effects—by restoring freedom of competition and individual coordination of prices and wages.

The Keynesians think in terms of aggregates. Their remedy is to increase the total money supply, and thereby to bring the price "level" sufficiently above the wage "level" to restore or maintain profit margins and so keep the wheels of industry spinning at full speed.

This remedy is defective in two respects. It tacitly assumes that there is a *uniform* discrepancy between prices and wages and a *uniform* percentage of "idle capacity" throughout industry. Neither is true. If "industry" is estimated to be operating at 80 per cent of capacity, we must remember that this figure is at best an *average*. It may cover a situation in which, say, industry A is operating at only 60 per cent, industry B at 63 per cent, and so on up to industry M at 97 per cent and industry N at 100 per cent. If we try to expand the money supply enough to return industries A and B to full capacity, we may completely "overheat" industries M and N and produce serious productive distortions and bottlenecks.

What is more, an increase in the stock of money, contrary to Keynesian theory, will begin to force an irregular increase in prices long before "full capacity" has been reached and the "slack" taken up—if only for the reason that the "slack" is never unifrom throughout industry. In a very short time, also, with the increase in

prices and the increase in the demand for labor, wages
will start climbing too. Then, if the previous trouble was
that most wages were already too high in relation to
most prices, there will again be discoordination between wages and prices; and the Keynesian prescrip-
tion will call for still further doses of government
spending, deficits, and new money.

So the Keynesian medicine must lead to chronic deficits and chronic inflating of the money supply. This is
precisely what we have had. It is no accident that we
have just run eight annual deficits in succession, and
that we have had 32 deficits in the last 38 years. It is no
accident that the U. S. money supply (currency plus
demand deposits) has been increased more than fivefold—from $36 billion at the end of 1939 to $199 billion
in September, 1969. And so it is no accident that, in
spite of a tremendous increase in industrial production
in this thirty-year period, consumer prices have increased (to June, 1969) by 164 per cent.

Today the Federal Government is spending in a single year *269 times as much* as in the fiscal year before
the outbreak of World War I. The recent increase in
annual spending is being attributed by government
spokesmen to the cost of the war in Vietnam. Yet
though in 1970 scheduled national defense expenditures are $35.6 billion greater than in 1960, total expen-
ditures are $103.1 billion greater. This means that
non-defense expenditures alone have increased $67.5
billion in the same period. It is not the war, but the
determination to impose the welfare state, that has led
to this incredible squandering.

A central fallacy of Keynesianism, as of all inflationary nostrums, is that they chronically confuse "income"
in terms of paper money with real income in goods and
services. It is possible to increase paper-money income
to any amount by debasing the currency. But real in-

come can only be increased by working harder or more
efficiently, saving more, investing more, and producing
more.

So let us not be too impressed by politicians who
constantly cite the increase in dollar incomes, in dollar
"gross national product," to show that we never had it
so good. In Italy today, as a result of past inflations, it
takes 624 lire to buy an American dollar. So anyone in
Italy with an annual income or even total property
worth more than $1,600 American dollars is already a
millionaire in his own currency.

/\/\/\/\

CHAPTER 3

"We Owe It To Ourselves"

AT THE OUTBREAK OF WORLD WAR I, THE NATIONAL debt amounted to only $1.2 billion. At the end of 1919 it had swelled because of that war to $25.5 billion. But there was a national sense of responsibility about it. Prudent policies were followed. Successive Republican administrations reduced it at a rate of nearly $1 billion a year, so that at the end of 1930 it was down to $16.2 billion.

But then, well before we got into World War II, welfare spending started to soar. There was no effort to balance the budget; the cult of deficits prevailed. At the end of fiscal year 1941, five months before Pearl Harbor, the public debt was at the then record level of $55.5 billion. We ended the war with a public debt of $260 billion, but this time there was no important reduction, except almost by accident in 1948 and 1951. Chronic deficits have now brought it up to $363 billion.

It is amusing to recall the rationalizations that accompanied each succeeding deficit. At first each presidential message would solemnly estimate a surplus for the next fiscal year, which always turned out to be a deficit before the year was over. Next, the budget was always to be balanced sometime in the next couple of years— but, of course, not now.

Then a new doctrine began to be put forward. It set up a straw-man: the conservative who allegedly insisted that the budget must be balanced every year, come hell or high water. Ah no, this new doctrine replied; the budget need be balanced only over a period. But the high priests of the new doctrine never got around to specifying just how long the period should be, or just when it would be safe to begin to show a surplus again. They showed no ardor for sticking to the arithmetic even of their own proposals. If, as in the eight years 1961 through 1968, there was an uninterrupted average administrative deficit of $8 billion a year, shouldn't there be an average surplus of $8 billion a year for the next eight years?

The argument for a budget balanced "over a period" has, in fact, been quietly dropped. In its place is the argument that the budget should *never* be balanced when there is less than full employment, or even when there threatens to be less than full employment. And this again has become in fact an argument for a perpetual deficit. For though President Johnson's economic advisers called for and got a tax increase (but never called for a spending cut), no one dreamed of suggesting a surplus, or even a balanced budget. In presenting his budget for the fiscal year 1968, for example, President Johnson planned a deficit of $4.3 billion

in the cash budget and of $8.1 billion in the orthodox
administrative budget. (The actual administrative deficit turned out to be $25.4 billion.) "To seek a *lower*
deficit or a surplus" for 1968, he warned, "would be
unwarranted and self-defeating" because it would "de-
press economic activity."

The implication of this whole philosophy is that it is
dangerous even to balance the budget, and that so far
from trying to pay off or even reduce the national debt,
we should permit a perpetual increase.

Let us look at what this has already meant for annual
interest payments alone. They have doubled in the last
ten years—from $8.3 billion in 1960 to $16 billion in
1970. Thus interest payments alone are every year
greater than the entire amount it took to run the government in 1941, and more than five times as much as
was required to run the government in 1929.

In 1932 Candidate Franklin Roosevelt was alarmed
because the national debt had increased by $3 billion
in the preceding two years. But for a generation the size
and growth of the national debt have been lightly dismissed with the argument that "we owe it to ourselves."
This was presented in the Nineteen Thirties as a brilliant discovery of the "new" economics; but the argument is so old that it was familiar to the great British
philosopher David Hume, who answered it in a brilliant
essay in 1740: "The practice of contracting debt will
almost infallibly be abused in every government . . .
We have indeed been told that the public is no weaker
upon account of its debts, since they are mostly due
among ourselves." But Hume then went on to point out
that the creditors who received the interest on the debt
were by no means the same people as the taxpayers
who had to pay it, and that practically no one paid and
received exactly the same amount. The tax burden fell
mainly upon the active workers and producers, and

hampered production. "If all our present taxes be mort-
gaged," he asked, "must we not invent new ones? And
may not this matter be carried to a length that is ruinous
and destructive?"

"I must confess," he also wrote in the course of his
essay, "that there is a strange supineness, from long
custom, creeped into all ranks of men, with regard to
public debts," so that hardly anyone dared to hope that
substantial progress would ever be made in paying
them off. We find plenty of evidence of this complacency today. Academic economists even vie with each
other in trying to prove that the situation is after all very
good.

A favorite argument of the last few years is that "the
nation is growing faster than its debt." This is "proved"
statistically. In the table below, for example, I merely
bring up to mid–1969 some comparisons presented (in
billions of dollars) by one academician in 1964:

	1945	1969
National debt	$260	$359
Gross National Product	$212	$925
Debt as burden on GNP	123%	39%

So we might advance triumphantly to the conclusion
that the national debt, when viewed as a burden on a
year's production, has been cut by two-thirds since
1945!

The conclusion would be technically correct, but
complacency would be unjustified. The reason the national debt is less of a burden is that, through inflation,
the purchasing power of the dollar has been steadily

reduced. It has been reduced 65 per cent since 1933
and more than 50 per cent since 1945. Let us state this
another way. By failing to balance its budget, by borrowing, by monetizing the debt, by printing more dollars, by steadily diluting the dollar's purchasing power,
the government has in effect repudiated 65 cents of
every dollar it borrowed in 1933 and 50 cents of every
dollar it borrowed in 1945.

To put it bluntly, the government's creditors have
been swindled.

Adam Smith, writing in 1776, was perfectly familiar
with this method of disguised repudiation. "When national debts have once been accumulated to a certain
degree," he wrote, "there is scarce, I believe, a single
instance of their having been fairly and completely
paid." But governments usually covered "the disgrace
of a real bankruptcy" by the "juggling trick" of "a pre-
tended payment" in depreciated money.

So the relationship that seems to give some present-
day writers so much satisfaction—that the national
debt, in dollar terms, has been falling in relation to the
gross national product in dollar terms—is simply the
outcome of the steady depreciation of the dollar. The
more inflation we have, and the more the purchasing
power of the dollar is depreciated, the more the national debt will "fall" in relation to the GNP, because
the GNP, measured in soaring prices, will rise in relation to the dollar debt.

Do we have any serious intention of ever paying off
our national debt in dollars of at least present purchasing power? If so, isn't it about time we begin to balance
the budget and make an honest start?

CHAPTER 4

Consequences of Dollar Debasement

˄˅˄˅˄˅˄˄˅˄˅˄˄˅˄˅˄˄˅˄˅˄˄˅˄˅˄˄˅˄˅˄˄˅˄˅˄˄

LET US BEGIN BY RECALLING TWO COMPARISONS already mentioned. From the end of 1939 to the end of 1968 the United States' stock of money (hand-to-hand currency plus demand bank deposits) has been increased more than fivefold—from $36 billion to $193 billion. In the same thirty-year period (in spite of a huge increase in industrial production), prices of goods and services increased by an average of 164 per cent.

This debasement of the dollar resulted in a succession of problems, including a chronic "deficit" in the American balance of payments.

The "balance-of-payments problem" has arisen not merely because of our domestic inflation but because of the combination of this with the so-called "gold exchange" standard and the world monetary system set up at Bretton Woods in 1944. Under that system each government undertook to keep its own currency unit within 1 per cent of parity in either direction by buying or selling that currency against other currencies in the foreign exchange market. In addition, the United States Government undertook to make the dollar the world's "reserve currency" and anchor currency by guaranteeing to keep it convertible at all times (for foreign central banks, but not for its own citizens) into gold at the fixed price of $35 an ounce.

Though only central banks, and neither American nor foreign private citizens, have the right to ask for this conversion, keeping the dollar convertible into gold at this fixed price has proved increasingly embarrassing to our monetary authorities, especially since 1957. During the last decade we have been sending or spending abroad for various purposes—to pay for imports, for foreign aid, and for the support of our armed forces in Europe and in Vietnam—billions of more dollars each year than we have been getting back in payment for our exports and earnings on our capital invested abroad.

This excess of outgoing dollars is called the "deficit" in our balance of payments. From the end of 1957 to the end of 1967 this deficit ran at an average of $2.8 billion a year. At the end of 1968 the cumulative total was in the neighborhood of $30 billion. In early 1969 the deficit on a "liquidity" basis was running at an annual rate of $6.8 billion.

As a result, our monetary gold stock had fallen from $22.8 billion at the end of 1957 to only $10.4 billion in July, 1969. Against these reduced gold reserves the United States had liquid liabilities to foreign official institutions of $10.8 billion, plus short-term liabilities to private foreigners of $22.6 billion—a total of nearly $34 billion.

In much discussion our dollar liabilities to private foreigners are not counted as a potential demand on our gold reserves because private banks, firms, and individuals cannot directly demand gold for their dollars. But under the International Monetary Fund agreements they can always indirectly sell their dollars at par to their respective central banks.

In sum, against United States gold reserves of only about $10 billion there are more than three times as many potential foreign dollar claims for gold.

As our gold has drained out, and as foreign dollar claims against it have mounted, the blame has been put on this "deficit" in our balance of payments. But instead of dealing with the main cause of this deficit—domestic inflation—our governmental authorities have allowed the inflation to go on, and have even increased it, while trying to stop the symptom. They have treated the deficit in the balance of payments as itself the problem, and have adopted desperate measures to try to halt it by direct controls.

Their first major control, imposed in 1964, was a penalty tax on purchases by Americans of foreign securities. To make such foreign investments the culprit responsible for a balance-of-payments deficit was not only arbitrary but implausible on its face. In the five years 1958 to 1962 the aggregate net outflow of $16.6 billion for new foreign investment was offset by $15.4 billion of income from previous investment. Even the Secretary of the Treasury, who had asked for the penalty tax, conceded: "In the long run the outflow of American capital to foreign countries is more than balanced by the inflow of income earned on that capital."

He urged the tax, in fact, "only as a temporary measure to meet our problem pending more fundamental solutions." Of course the more fundamental solutions were never adopted, so not only was the "temporary" security tax renewed, but on January 1, 1968, the President added mandatory controls on direct investments by American corporations abroad.

The implication of these measures is that our private foreign investment has been one of the chief causes of the deficit in our balance of payments. This is clearly untrue. It is Federal spending, through foreign aid and military outlays, that has been in deficit. In recent years the private sector as a whole, as a result of export surpluses and income on private investments abroad, has continued to generate a payments surplus.

In 1967 our total new foreign investments—including bank loans, purchases of foreign securities, and direct investments in factories and sales facilities—amounted to $5.6 billion. But the income from these and earlier private investments came to $6.2 billion.

At best, then, all these foreign investment restrictions and prohibitions are shortsighted. Any reduction we make in new foreign investment today means a corresponding reduction in investment income tomorrow.

If the Federal Government, instead of picking foreign investment as the culprit chiefly responsible for our balance-of-payments deficit, had put punitive tariffs on the further import of foreign luxuries—liquors, wines, perfumes, jewelry, furs, and automobiles—its action would still have been a mistake, but much less damaging to our future economic strength. These tight curbs on direct foreign investments by American corporations must severely hamper their ability to compete successfully with other international corporations in Europe and the rest of the world.

The President's own Economic Report of 1967 pointed out that: "U. S. investment abroad generates not only a flow of investment income but also additional U. S. exports. From a balance-of-payments point of view this is an additional dividend." The U. S. Department of

Commerce found, in fact, that in 1964 $6.3 billion, or 25 per cent of our total exports in that year, went to affiliates of American companies overseas.

It is hardly too much to say that direct foreign investments, with the exports and income to which they give rise, are the greatest single source of long-range strength in our balance-of-payments position.

Still worse, from the standpoint of their direct restriction on personal liberty, were the Johnson Administration's proposals (fortunately not enacted) to have Congress impose practically prohibitive penalty taxes on Americans travelling abroad.

The whole effort to eliminate our balance-of-payments deficit by direct controls over arbitrarily selected individual items is doomed to failure. Such controls may succeed in changing the relative amounts of different items, but cannot change the end result. At best we can make our immediate balance of payments look better at the expense of our future balance. We cannot unilaterally cut down our purchases or travel or investments abroad without also cutting down our sales abroad and our investment income from abroad. In his Economic Report of 1968, President Johnson himself conceded that "by provoking retaliation" we may "reduce our receipts by as much as or more than our payments."

The whole so-called "balance-of-payments problem" would never have arisen except under the arbitrarily contrived International Monetary Fund gold-exchange system set up at Bretton Woods in 1944. It could not exist if the United States and other countries were on a pure "floating" paper standard with rates fluctuating daily in a free market, because under such a system the fluctuations would themselves set in motion the self-correcting forces to prevent unwanted deficits or surpluses from arising. Nor could the balance-of-payments problem exist if the United States and other leading countries were on a full gold standard. A "deficit" in the balance of payments would then lead to an immediate outflow of gold. This in turn would lead to immediately higher interest rates and a contraction of currency and credit in the "deficit" country, and the opposite results in the "surplus" countries, and so bring the so-called deficit to a halt.

Under the Bretton Woods system and the "gold exchange" standard, however, no self-correction of this sort is allowed to take place. When we "lose" paper dollars abroad we simply print more at home to take their place. And when Europe gains these dollars they find their way into the central banks, where they become additional "reserves" against which the European governments issue still more of their own currency. Thus further inflation, in both the "deficit" and the "surplus" country, seems to take place automatically.

In the IMF system there are no freely fluctuating market rates for individual currencies to reveal and correct international imbalances. Market rates are not allowed to fluctuate by more than 1 per cent above or below parity. At that point each government is obligated to buy or sell its own or foreign currencies to prevent any further departure from parity.

These currency-pegging operations are supplemented by the so-called gold-exchange standard. This arrangement, which goes back to international agreements in 1921 and 1922, permits central banks to count not only their gold but their holdings of dollars (and of British pounds) as part of their reserves. The arrangement was adopted in the belief that there was a "shortage of gold" and a "shortage of international liquidity." As a result the world's monetary "reserves" today consist of about $42 billion in gold *plus* about $28 billion of "reserve currencies," of which more than $15 billion are

American dollars. As credit and other currencies are issued against these reserve currencies, the reserves themselves are inflated.

The real reason the American monetary authorities fear a continued "deficit" in the balance of payments is that they have given the central banks of other countries the right to demand gold for their dollars at $35 an ounce. They have seen more than half our gold reserves flow out in the last twelve years, and they are fearful of losing any more.

They long ago persuaded the Federal Government to prohibit American citizens from holding or asking for gold. In the last few years they have resorted to increasingly desperate expedients. Where possible, they have brought political pressure on foreign central banks to keep them from asking for gold for their dollars. Early in 1968 they stopped feeding out gold to hold down the price in private markets in London, Paris, and Zurich. They now try to maintain an inherently unstable two-price system, with official monetary gold at $35 an ounce and non-monetary gold free to sell at whatever price supply and demand fix.

Early in 1968 the Administration also got Congress to abolish the remaining gold-reserve requirement of 25 per cent against Federal Reserve notes, on the plea that this was necessary to reassure foreign central banks by making all remaining United States gold holdings available to them. But what this action really did was to remove the last legal limitation on the amount of paper money that the Federal Reserve system may issue.

Finally, the American government has pressed for the creation by the International Monetary Fund of "special drawing rights" (SDR's), or "paper gold," to "supplement" dollars as international reserves. The only thing this purposely complicated scheme can do is to adulterate reserves still further and make it possible for nations to issue still more paper money against these paper SDR's, which are declared with a straight face to be just as good as gold if not better.

All these schemes are unsound, and in the end all of them will prove futile. The truth is that no solution of the monetary problem, national or international, will be possible until inflation is stopped, and that it will not be stopped as long as we have the welfare state.

/\/\.\/\.\/\.\

CHAPTER 5

The High Cost of Wage Hikes

/\

IT OUGHT TO BE OBVIOUS THAT MINIMUM WAGE laws hurt most the very people they are designed to "protect." When a law exists that no one is to be paid less than $64 for a 40-hour week, then no one whose services are not worth $64 a week to an employer will be employed at all. We cannot make a man worth a given amount by making it illegal for anyone to offer him less. We merely deprive him of the right to earn the amount that his abilities and opportunities would permit him to earn, while we deprive the community of the moderate services he is capable of rendering. In brief, for a low wage we substitute unemployment.

Yet we initiated the folly of a Federal minimum wage law 30 years ago, and we have been compounding that folly ever since. The first Labor Standards Act of 1938 fixed a minimum wage of 25 cents an hour. This was raised to 30 cents in 1939, 40 cents in 1945, 75 cents in January, 1950, $1.00 in March, 1956, $1.15 in September, 1961, $1.25 in September, 1963, $1.40 in February, 1967, and $1.60 in February, 1968.

In 1938 the average hourly wage in manufacturing industries was 62 cents an hour. In January, 1968, it was $2.64 an hour. But our legislators, not content with this general rise in wages due to more and better tools and natural economic forces, have decided to keep raising the legal minimum wage even faster than the fast-rising market average. Thus the statutory minimum was only 29 per cent of average hourly earnings in manufacturing just before the increase in 1950, but 40 per cent before the increase of the minimum in 1956, 43 per cent before the increase in 1961, 47 per cent before the increase in 1963, and 54 per cent before the increase in 1968. The consequence of this is that the legal minimum wage was pushed up 114 per cent between early 1956 and 1968, though average hourly earnings in manufacturing rose only 55 per cent. Meanwhile, the Federal minimum wage has become effective over a far greater range.

The net result of all this has been to force up the wage rates of unskilled labor much more than those of skilled labor. A result of this, in turn, has been that though an increasing shortage has developed in skilled labor, the proportion of unemployed among the unskilled, among teen-agers, females and non-whites has been growing.

The outstanding victim has been the Negro, and particularly the Negro teen-ager. In 1952, the unemployment rate among white teen-agers and non-white teen-agers was the same—9 per cent. But year by year, as the minimum wage has been jacked higher and higher, a disparity has grown and increased. In February of 1968, the unemployment rate among white teen-agers was 11.6 per cent, but among non-white teen-agers it had soared to 26.6 per cent.

In addition to the direct harm done by the minimum wage in creating unemployment among the unskilled, it must bear at least part of the blame for the recent riots in the cities—where the unemployed are concentrated.

The statistical evidence showing that the minimum wage has caused unemployment among Negroes and the unskilled is extensive. It is gratifying to report that some of the country's outstanding academic economists —Professors Yale Brozen, Arthur Burns, Milton Fried-man, Gottfried Haberler, James Tobin, to mention a few —have gathered this evidence and presented a conclu-sive case against a statutory minimum wage. Yet succes-sive Administrations and Congresses have persistently refused to accept their logic or to face the glaring facts.

There are other labor laws, antedating the minimum wage, that have had even worse consequences. In the early Nineteen Thirties the theory grew up that wages were too low and workers were exploited because there were not enough unions and those that existed had too little bargaining power. The proposed remedy for this was to create more and stronger unions, and the way to do that was to forbid employers to discriminate against union workers in hiring, in promoting, or in granting wage increases. Therefore, in 1935 Congress passed the Wagner Act, which gave unions the right to "bargain collectively through representatives of their own choosing" and prohibited employers from engaging in a whole list of "unfair labor practices."

The Wagner Act was completely one-sided, hypo-critical, and self-contradictory. On the one hand, it pre-tended to be two-sided by making it an unfair labor practice "by discrimination in regard to hire or tenure of employment or any term or condition of employment to *encourage or discourage* membership in any labor organization." But immediately following this was a provision declaring that "nothing in this act . . . shall preclude an employer from making an agreement with a labor organization. . . to require as a condition of employment membership therein." In brief, the law prohibited an employer from discriminating against union members, but permitted and encouraged (and often in fact compelled) him to discriminate against non-union members.

The Wagner Act proved so viciously one-sided in practice that in 1947 Congress amended it in the Taft-Hartley Act. But the Taft-Hartley Act, contrary to popular impression, changed little of substance. And the National Labor Relations Board has successfully ignored or circumvented the provisions that did.

The factual situation today is that the compulsory union shop can be forced on employers and workers in the majority of the states. If a union makes an exorbitant demand, the employer cannot simply refuse to meet it. He is compelled by the Taft-Hartley Act to keep "bargaining" with that union and no one else. If he announces that he will regard strikers as having quit their jobs, and will carry on his business by hiring workers to replace them, his plant will be surrounded by pickets to intimidate anyone who thinks of passing through. And because of the legal roadblocks set up by the Norris-LaGuardia Act of 1932, he will probably be unable to get injunctive relief in the courts, even from crippling vandalism and violence.

The "right to strike" is interpreted today not merely as the right to quit work, but the "right" forcibly to prevent others from taking the jobs that the strikers have voluntarily vacated. The Taft-Hartley Act, amending the Wagner Act, specifically provided that "to bargain collectively . . . does not compel either party to

agree to a proposal or require the making of a conces-
sion." But the employer is in fact compelled to make
concessions. He is compelled to make them because
unions today enjoy a special license to keep a plant
closed by intimidatory mass picketing until their demands are met. If an employer does somehow succeed
in keeping his plant open, and peaceably replacing
strikers to carry on his business, the Labor Board is
likely to come along years later, as it has done time and
time again, and rule that by finally ceasing to "bargain"
with the original union that struck he violated the Taft-
Hartley Act and must therefore re-employ the original
strikers, with retroactive pay to cover the period of
their unemployment.

Yet this factual situation is ignored by practically everybody as if it did not exist. When a particularly outra-
geous or disruptive strike halts vital services, and a few
congressmen begin to demand compulsory arbitration,
they are told that the government should not intervene
but allow the processes of "free collective bargaining"
to continue.

It is true that compulsory arbitration is not the solution. But it is not true that the "collective bargaining"
taking place is "free." The government is in fact inter-
vening every day through its one-sided laws. It is already a participant on the side of the striking union. It
is granting special immunities to the union to use intimidation and violence. It is putting special compulsions on
the employer to yield to the demands of the union, or
to grant costly concessions, for fear of the even more
costly or perhaps mortal penalties if he breaks off
negotiations with the union members on strike and de-
cides to employ replacements.

By the Norris-LaGuardia Act of 1932, by the Wagner
Act of 1935 and the Taft-Hartley amendments of 1947,
by loaded decisions pouring out daily from the National

Labor Relations Board, and by the failure of local authorities to provide adequate police protection to employers and workers trying peaceably to carry on a
struck business, we are daily forcing up wage rates to
points that threaten to bring the economy to a halt,
unless more money is printed so that demand, prices,
and profit-margins can keep pace.

For thirty years we have been in an unending race
between the printing press and the demands of the
labor unions. Instead of showing any signs of slowing to
a halt, the race is becoming more determined and more
desperate on both sides.

/\\.\\/\\.\\/\\.\\/\\.\\/\\

CHAPTER 6

Price Controls

/\\.\\/\\.\\/\\.\\/\\.\\/\\.\\/\\.\\/\\.\\/\\.\\/\\.\\/\\.\\/\\.\\/\\.\\/\\.\\/\\.\\/\\.\\/\\.\\/\\

WHEN THE WELFARE STATE SPENDS RECKLESSLY, runs chronic deficits, expands credit, and prints more money, prices begin to soar. Invariably the government blames business, especially Big Business, and hints darkly at price controls.

But being a self-styled "liberal" government, it begins by suggesting only "voluntary" controls. It draws up "guidelines." Prices of course continue to rise, because the government is printing more money, thereby reducing the value of the currency unit.

The government's next step is to select as its special target some big corporation (or industry consisting mainly of big corporations) and demand that it roll back some price increase it has just announced. The big corporation is selected for attack, of course, because it is easy to arouse popular prejudice against it. It can either be denounced as a monopoly or accused of "administering" prices.

The favorite scapegoat in the United States for the last twenty years or more has been the steel industry. Though the total value of the steel produced yearly in this country amounts to only 2 per cent of the gross national product, the government, whenever it attacks steel prices, contends that steel enters into a multitude of products, that a steel price increase is "pyramided" throughout industry, and so sets off a chain reaction of inflation. This argument will not bear serious analysis, but that has never prevented its repeated use.

One minor irony is that though the government publishes a monthly index of consumer prices, and a monthly index of wholesale prices, and that though the former is a weighted average of some 400 selected prices and the latter a weighted average of some 2,000 prices, the monthly government report never tells the reader just how many of these prices rose and how many fell in the month reported. It is true that it sometimes gives partial enumerations. Thus, in its report on wholesale prices for March, 1968, it tells us: "Prices were higher for 110 of the 225 industrial product classes; there was no change for 85 and declines occurred for 30." But if it told us that of the 2,000 individual prices it records of all items, about 1,000, say, went up in a given month, 740 were unchanged and 260 declined, the public would instantly see the absurdity as well as the injustice of the government's selecting one price rise among 1,000 price rises, or even a price rise in one industry out of price rises in 110 industries, for special denunciation and attack.

A rise of nearly all prices, or of most prices out of tens of thousands, indicates the operation of a common cause. That cause is the monetary policies of the government itself. Prices do not rise today because businessmen have suddenly become greedier than they were yesterday. We may assume that sellers operating either under competition or monopoly were already charging as much as they could successfully get. The problem is to explain why they can charge more today than they did yesterday, or more this year than last year. If nearly all can charge more, this means that some general condition has changed.

Government price control attempts to ignore this change. That is why government price control always works harm. Attempts to hold down or roll back prices, when they do not merely lead to black markets and quality deterioration, must reduce and disrupt production and distort the balance and structure of production. (Artificially depressed prices, of course, also stimulate demand for the items subject to them.)

When the price of one item, say some necessity such as bread or milk, is held below the price that supply and demand would set in a free market, it reduces the comparative profit margin in making that product and soon creates a shortage of that product. This is exactly the opposite result from the one the government price-fixers had in mind. If, in the effort to cure this, the government tries to hold down the prices of the labor, raw materials, and other factors that go into producing the price-controlled product, the price control must be extended in ever-widening circles, until the government finds itself trying to fix the price of everything.

As there are probably at least 10 million separate prices in the American economy, and as this implies something on the order of 50 *trillion* cross-relationships among prices, the government sets itself a fantastically impossible task. But this does not mean it cannot do immense harm to the economy when it nevertheless undertakes this task.

It is ironic that even a "labor" government, once it

undertakes price controls to try to prevent the consequences of its own monetary inflation, is finally forced to face the fact that it cannot do this unless it is also prepared to control and hold down wages. This is what happened in England. But a government's wage-control orders are enormously harder to enforce than its price-control orders. If the wage control is real and rigid, the unions simply defy it; so it finally becomes riddled with loopholes and exceptions, which cause the price control either to do increasing damage to production or to break down.

A special case of price control is the attempt to hold down interest rates, either on loans to business or on home mortgages. At the beginning this looks easier than other forms of price control. It merely seems necessary to issue more money to increase the supply of loanable funds. But when interest rates are reduced in this way, two consequences follow. The lower interest encourages more borrowing, which tends to raise the rate again. And the increased amount of money and credit starts pushing up prices and wages. This forces businessmen to borrow still more, if they want to continue to buy even the same volume of inventories and employ even the same number of workers as before, to do the same volume of business.

And if, as a result of the increased volume of money and credit, prices have risen, say, 5 per cent in the last twelve months and are expected to rise 6 per cent in the next twelve months, lenders begin to realize that when they get 6 per cent nominal interest on their money they are in reality getting no interest at all.

This is one reason why interest rates in the United States in 1968 and 1969 soared to record high levels. It is precisely the government effort to hold them down that forced them up. This is just one more illustration of how government controls eventually bring about precisely the opposite effects of those intended.

Arthur M. Okun, the last chairman of President Johnson's Council of Economic Advisers, ignoring the fact that unions cannot successfully raise wages or businessmen prices unless monetary inflation permits it, called on business and labor to practice "voluntary restraint" and stop raising prices and wages. But if employers and workers did exercise "voluntary restraint," and deliberately charged less or asked less than they could get in a free competitive market, they would in fact be doing the community a disservice.

The demand and supply of each of thousands of different commodities and services are changing every day. When an increase in the money supply does not falsify the result, the goods and services in most demand rise in price while those in least demand fall. So the profit margin in supplying the goods in greater demand increases while that in supplying the goods in less demand falls. This causes more to be produced of the goods in more demand and relatively less to be produced of the goods in less demand. Thus the tens of thousands of different goods and services produced in the nation tend constantly to be produced in the changing proportions in which they are most wanted.

Prices are indispensable signals to producers and consumers. They must tell the truth about supply and demand. "Voluntary restraints"—and still more, government "guidelines"—falsify the signals and disorganize and unbalance production.

Monetary inflation is a dreadful thing. But what does immensely more harm than the inflation itself is the attempt to conceal or suppress its consequences through price and wage controls.

CHAPTER 7

More on Price Controls

THE WELFARE STATE CAN ARISE AND PERSIST ONLY
by cultivating and living on a set of economic delusions
in the minds of the voters.

As we saw at the beginning of the last chapter, the
policies of the welfare state follow a typical time se-
quence. First the welfare state promises special subsidies or other benefits to this or that pressure group. This
increases its expenditures. But it cannot or dare not
boost taxes enough to meet these increased expenditures fully. So it runs a deficit, and pays for it by printing
more irredeemable paper money. This lowers the value
of the currency unit by causing more money to be offered for the same supply of goods. The result is a price
rise. The next step of the inflating government is to

blame the price rise on sellers, on Big Business, on "profiteers." The step after that is to put legal ceilings on prices, or to order them to be rolled back, to "protect the consumer."

If the public is convinced, on the other hand, that it is the government's fiscal and monetary policies, and not the greed of producers and sellers, that are forcing up prices, and if the public realizes further that government price control only compounds the evils brought about by monetary inflation, and if the public recognizes that price control in the long run cannot help but must hurt the great body of consumers, then the chief political prop of the welfare state will collapse.

It is of the first importance, therefore, even if this necessitates some repetition, to consider the case against price controls in more detail and at much greater length than we did in the brief survey in the last chapter.

Prices in a free market are determined by supply and demand. If the relative demand for a product increases, consumers will be willing to pay more for it. Their competitive bids will both oblige them individually to pay more for it and enable producers to get more for it. This will raise the profit margins of the producers of that product. This, in turn, will tend to attract more firms into the manufacture of that product, and induce existing firms to invest more capital into making it. The increased production will tend to reduce the price of the product again, and to reduce the profit margin in making it. The increased investment in new manufacturing equipment may lower the cost of production. Or —particularly if we are concerned with some extractive industry such as petroleum, gold, silver, or copper—the increased demand and output may raise the cost of production. In any case, the price will have a definite effect on demand, output, and cost of production, just as these in turn will affect price. All four—demand, supply, cost, and price—are interrelated. A change in one will bring changes in the others.

Connexity of Prices

Just as the demand, supply, cost, and price of any single commodity are all interrelated, so are the prices of all commodities related to each other. These relationships are both direct and indirect. Copper mines may yield silver as a by-product. This is connectedness, or connexity, of production. If the price of copper goes too high, consumers may substitute aluminum for many uses. This is a connexity of substitution. Dacron and cotton are both used in drip-dry shirts; this is a connexity of consumption.

In addition to these relatively direct connections among prices, there is an inescapable interconnectedness, or interconnexity, of all prices. One general factor of production—labor—can be diverted, in the short run or in the long run, directly or indirectly, from one line into any other line. If one commodity goes up in price, and consumers are unwilling or unable to substitute another, they will be forced to consume a little less of something else. All products are in competition for the consumer's dollar; and a change in any one price will affect an indefinite number of other prices.

No single price, therefore, can be considered an isolated object in itself. It is interrelated with all other prices. It is precisely through these interrelationships that society is able to solve the immensely difficult and always changing problem of how to allocate production among thousands of different commodities and services so that each may be supplied as nearly as possible in relation to the comparative urgency of the need or desire for it.

As the eminent economist Ludwig von Mises has demonstrated, only the capitalist system, with private property, a sound currency, free markets, and freedom from price controls, can solve this great problem of "economic calculation."

Because the desire and need for, and the supply and cost of, every individual commodity or service are constantly changing, prices and price relationships are constantly changing. They are changing yearly, monthly, weekly, daily, hourly. People who think that prices normally rest at some fixed point, or can be easily held to some "right" level, could profitably spend an hour watching the ticker tape of the stock market, or reading the daily report in the newspapers of what happened yesterday in the foreign exchange market, and in the markets for coffee, cocoa, sugar, wheat, corn, rice, and eggs; cotton, hides, wool, and rubber; copper, silver, lead, and zinc. They will find that none of these prices ever stands still. This is why the constant attempts of governments to lower, raise, or freeze a particular price, or to freeze the interrelationship of wages and prices just where it was on a given date ("holding the line") are bound to be disruptive wherever they are not futile.

Efforts to Boost Prices

Let us begin by considering governmental efforts to keep prices up, or to raise them. Governments most frequently try to do this for commodities that constitute a principal item of export from their countries. Thus Japan once did it for silk and the British Empire for natural rubber; Brazil has done it and still periodically does it for coffee; and the United States has done it and still does it for cotton and wheat. The theory is that raising the price of these export commodities can only

do good and no harm domestically because it will raise
the incomes of domestic producers and do it almost
wholly at the expense of the foreign consumers.

All of these schemes follow a typical course. It is soon
discovered that the price of the commodity cannot be
raised unless the supply is first reduced. This may lead
in the beginning to the imposition of acreage restrictions. But the higher price gives an incentive to producers to increase their average yield per acre by planting
the supported product only on their most productive
acres, and by more intensive employment of fertilizers,
irrigation, and labor. When the government discovers
that this is happening, it turns to imposing absolute
quantitative controls on each producer. This is usually
based on each producer's previous production over a
series of years. The result of this quota system is to keep
out all new competition; to lock all existing producers
into their previous relative position, and therefore to
keep production costs high by removing the chief
mechanisms and incentives for reducing such costs.
The necessary readjustments are prevented from taking place.

Meanwhile, however, market forces are still functioning in foreign countries. Foreigners object to paying the
higher price. They cut down their purchases of the
valorized commodity from the valorizing country, and
search for other sources of supply. The higher price
gives an incentive to other countries to start producing
the valorized commodity. Thus, the British rubber
scheme led Dutch producers to increase rubber production in Dutch dependencies. This not only lowered
rubber prices, but caused the British to lose permanently their previous monopolistic position. In addition,
the British scheme aroused resentment in the United
States, the chief consumer, and stimulated the eventually successful development of synthetic rubber. In the
same way, without going into detail, Brazil's coffee

schemes and America's cotton schemes gave both a
political and a price incentive to other countries to initi-
ate or increase production of coffee and cotton, and
both Brazil and the United States lost their previous
monopolistic positions.

Meanwhile, at home, all these schemes require the
setting up of an elaborate system of controls and an
elaborate bureaucracy to formulate and enforce them.
These have to be elaborate, because each individual
producer must be controlled. An illustration of what
happens may be found in the United States Department of Agriculture. In 1929, before most of the crop
control schemes came into being, there were 24,000
persons employed in the Department of Agriculture.
Today there are 120,000. These enormous bureaucra-
cies, of course, always have a vested interest in finding
reasons why the controls they were hired to enforce
should be continued and expanded. And of course
these controls restrict the individual's liberty and set
precedents for still further restrictions.

None of these consequences seems to discourage
government efforts to boost prices of certain products
above what would otherwise be their competitive market level. We still have international coffee agreements
and international wheat agreements. A particular irony
is that the United States was among the sponsors in
organizing the international coffee agreement, though
its people are the chief consumers of coffee and therefore the most immediate victims of the agreement.
Another irony is that the United States imposes *import*
quotas on sugar, which necessarily discriminate in favor
of some sugar-exporting nations and therefore against
others. These quotas force all American consumers to
pay higher prices for sugar in order that a tiny minority
of American sugar cane producers can get higher
prices.

I need not point out that these attempts to "stabilize"

or raise prices of primary agricultural products *politi-
calize* every price and production decision and create
friction among nations.

Holding Prices Down

Now let us turn to governmental efforts to *lower*
prices or at least to keep them from rising. These efforts
occur repeatedly in most nations, not only in wartime,
but in any time of inflation. The typical process is something like this: The government, for whatever reason,
follows policies that increase the quantity of money and
credit. This inevitably starts pushing up prices. But
higher prices are not popular with consumers. Therefore the government promises that it will "hold the
line" against further price increases.

Let us say it begins with bread and milk and other
necessities. The first thing that happens, assuming that
the government can enforce its decrees, is that the
profit margin in producing necessities falls, or is elimi-
nated, for marginal producers, while the profit margin
in producing luxuries is unchanged or goes higher. As
we saw in the previous chapter, this reduces and dis-
courages the production of the controlled necessities
and relatively encourages the increased production of
luxuries. But this is exactly the opposite result from
what the price controllers had in mind. If the government then tries to prevent this discouragement to the
production of the controlled commodities by keeping
down the cost of the raw materials, labor and other
factors of production that go into those commodities, it
must start controlling prices and wages in ever-widening circles until it is finally trying to control the price of
everything.

But if it tries to do this thoroughly and consistently,

it will find itself trying to control literally millions of prices and trillions of price cross-relationships. It will be fixing rigid allocations and quotas for each producer and for each consumer. Of course these controls will have to extend in detail to both importers and exporters.

Price Control Distorts Production

If a government continues to create more currency with one hand while rigidly holding down prices with the other, it will do immense harm. And let us note also that even if the government is not inflating the currency, but tries to hold either absolute or relative prices just where they were, or has instituted an "income policy" or "wage policy" drafted in accordance with some mechanical formula, it will do increasingly serious harm. For in a free market, even when the so-called price "level" is not changing, all prices are constantly changing in relation to each other. They are responding to changes in costs of production, of supply, and of demand for each commodity or service.

And these price changes, both absolute and relative, are in the overwhelming main both necessary and desirable. For they are drawing capital, labor, and other resources out of the production of goods and services that are less wanted and into the production of goods and services that are more wanted. They are adjusting the balance of production to the unceasing changes in demand. They are producing thousands of goods and services in the relative amounts in which they are socially wanted. These relative amounts are changing every day. Therefore the market adjustments and price and wage incentives that lead to these adjustments must be changing every day.

Price control always reduces, unbalances, distorts, and discoordinates production. Price control becomes progressively harmful with the passage of time. Even a fixed price or price relationship that may be "right" or "reasonable" on the day it is set can become increasingly unreasonable or unworkable.

What governments never realize is that, so far as any individual commodity is concerned, the cure for high prices is high prices. High prices lead to economy in consumption and stimulate and increase production. Both of these results increase supply and tend to bring prices down again.

Excessive Fears of Monopoly

Very well, someone may say; so government price control in many cases is harmful. But so far you have been talking as if the market were governed by perfect competition. But what of monopolistic markets? What of markets in which prices are controlled or fixed by huge corporations? Must not the government intervene here, if only to enforce competition or to bring about the price that real competition would bring if it existed?

The fears of most economists concerning the evils of "monopoly" have been unwarranted and certainly excessive. In the first place, it is very difficult to frame a satisfactory definition of economic monopoly. If there is only a single drug store, barber shop, or grocery in a small isolated town (and this is a typical situation), this store may be said to be enjoying a monopoly in that town. Again, everybody may be said to enjoy a monopoly of his own particular qualities or talents. Yehudi Menuhin has a monopoly of Menuhin's violin playing; Picasso of producing Picasso paintings; Elizabeth Taylor of her particular beauty and sex appeal; and so for lesser qualities and talents in every line.

On the other hand, nearly all economic monopolies are limited by the possibility of substitution. If copper piping is priced too high, consumers can substitute iron or plastics; if beef is too high, consumers can substitute lamb; if the original girl of your dreams rejects you, you can always marry somebody else. Thus, nearly every person, producer, or seller may enjoy a quasi monopoly within certain inner limits, but very few sellers are able to exploit that monopoly beyond certain outer limits. There has been a growing literature within recent years deploring the absence of perfect competition; there could have been equal emphasis on the absence of perfect monopoly. In real life competition is never perfect, but neither is monopoly.

Unable to find many examples of perfect monopoly, some economists have frightened themselves in recent years by conjuring up the specter of "oligopoly," the competition of the few. But they have come to their alarming conclusions only by inserting in their own *hypotheses* all sorts of imaginary secret agreements or tacit understandings between large producing units, and deducing what the results could be.

Now the mere *number* of competitors in a particular industry may have very little to do with the existence of effective competition. If General Electric and Westinghouse effectively compete, if General Motors and Ford and Chrysler effectively compete, if the Chase Manhattan and the First National City Bank of New York effectively compete, and so on (and no person who has had direct experience with these great companies can doubt that they dominantly do), then the result for consumers, not only in price but in quality of product or service, is not only as good as that which would be brought about by atomistic competition but much better, because consumers have the advantage of large-scale economies, and of large-scale research and development that small companies could not afford.

A Strange Numbers Game

The oligopoly theorists have had a baneful influence on the American antitrust division and on court decisions. The prosecutors and the courts have recently been playing a strange numbers game. In 1965, for example, a Federal district court held that a merger that had taken place between two New York City banks four years previously had been illegal, and must now be dissolved. The combined bank was not the largest in the city, but only the third largest; the merger had in fact enabled the bank to compete more effectively with its two larger competitors; its combined assets were still only one-eighth of those represented by all the banks of the city; and the merger itself had reduced the number of separate banks in New York from 71 to 70. (I should add that in the four years since the merger the number of *branch* bank offices in New York City has *increased* from 645 to 698.) The court agreed with the bank's lawyers that "the general public and small business have benefited" from bank mergers in the city. Nevertheless, the court continued, "practices harmless in themselves, or even those conferring benefits upon the community, cannot be tolerated when they tend to create a monopoly; those which restrict competition are unlawful no matter how beneficent they may be."

It is a strange thing, incidentally, that though politicians and the courts think it necessary to forbid an existing merger in order to increase the number of banks in a city from 70 to 71, they have no such insistence on big numbers in competition when it comes to political parties. The dominant American theory is that just two political parties are enough to give the American voter a real choice; that when there are more than these it merely causes confusion, and the people are not really served. There is much truth in this political theory as applied in the economic realm. If they are really competing, only two firms in an industry are enough to create effective competition.

Monopolistic Pricing

The real problem is not whether or not there is "monopoly" in a market, but whether there is monopolistic pricing. A monopoly price can arise when the responsiveness of demand is such that the monopolist can obtain a higher net income by selling a smaller quantity of his product at a higher price than by selling a larger quantity at a lower price. It is assumed that in this way the monopolist can realize a higher price than would have prevailed under "pure competition."

The theory that there can be such a thing as a monopoly price, higher than a competitive price would have been, is certainly valid. The real question is, how *useful* is this theory either to the supposed monopolist in deciding his price policies or to the legislator, prosecutor, or court in framing antimonopoly policies? The monopolist, to be able to exploit his position, must know what the "demand curve" *is* for his product. He does not know; he can only guess; he must try to find out by trial and error. And it is not merely the unemotional price response of the consumers that the monopolist must keep in mind; it is what the effect of his pricing policies will probably be in gaining the good will or arousing the resentment of the consumer. More importantly, the monopolist must consider the effect of his pricing policies in either encouraging or discouraging the entrance of competitors into the field. He may actually decide that his wisest policy in the long run would be to fix a price no higher than he thinks pure competition would set.

In any case, in the absence of competition, no one *knows* what the "competitive" price would be if it existed. Therefore, no one knows exactly how much higher an existing "monopoly" price is than a "competitive" price would be, and no one can be sure whether it is higher at all!

Yet antitrust policy, in the United States, at least, assumes that the courts can know how much an alleged monopoly or "conspiracy" price is above the competitive price that might have been. For when there is an alleged conspiracy to fix prices, purchasers are encouraged to sue to recover three times the amount they were allegedly forced to "overpay."

Refrain from Price Fixing

Our analysis leads us to the conclusion that governments should refrain, wherever possible, from trying to fix either maximum or minimum prices for anything. Where they have nationalized any service—the post office or the railroads, the telephone or electric power —they will of course have to establish pricing policies. And where they have granted monopolistic franchises —for subways, railroads, telephone or power companies—they will of course have to consider what price restrictions they will impose.

As to antimonopoly policy, whatever the present condition may be in other countries, in the United States this policy shows hardly a trace of consistency. It is uncertain, discriminatory, retroactive, capricious, and shot through with contradictions. No company today, even a moderate-sized company, can know when it will be held to have violated the antitrust laws, or why. It all depends on the economic bias of a particular public prosecutor, court, or judge.

There is immense hypocrisy about the subject. Politicians make eloquent speeches against "monopoly." Then they will impose tariffs and import quotas intended to protect monopoly and keep out competition; they will grant monopolistic franchises to bus companies or telephone companies; they will approve monopolistic patents and copyrights; they will try to control agricultural production to permit monopolistic farm prices. Above all, they will not only permit but impose labor monopolies on employers, and legally compel employers to "bargain" with these monopolies; and they will even allow these monopolies to impose their conditions by physical intimidation and coercion.

I suspect that the intellectual situation and the political climate in this respect are not much different in other countries. To work our way out of the existing legal chaos is, of course, a task for jurists as well as for economists. I have one modest suggestion: We can get a great deal of help from the old common law, which forbids fraud, misrepresentation, and all *physical* intimidation and coercion. "The end of the law," as John Locke reminded us in the seventeenth century, "is not to abolish or restrain, but to preserve and enlarge freedom." And so we can say today that in the economic realm the aim of the law should be not to constrict, but to maximize price freedom and market freedom.

/\./\./\./\

CHAPTER 8

Who Protects the Consumer?

/\.

CONSUMERS ARE SOMETIMES ASKED TO PAY TOO
much for goods. This has been true since the beginning
of time. Their great protection against overcharging has
been competition. The intelligent shopper can com-
pare price and quality, and go to the merchant who
offers the best goods at the cheapest price.

Consumers are sometimes cheated. This also has
been true since the beginning of time. They have sometimes been the victims of deceptive practices; they
have been sold shoddy goods, or defective goods, or
goods that have been misrepresented. Again, their
greatest protection has always been competition. They
can cease to buy from the dishonest merchant. In addition, when the amount involved is large enough, they

have been able under general laws against dishonest practices to resort to the law or to take a case to court.

But in recent years, particularly in the Kennedy and Johnson Administrations, an ominous network of legislation has grown up which attempts to regulate quality and quantity in the minutest detail in one industry or trade after another.

An idea of the scope of this can be gathered from a single message to Congress by President Johnson on February 17, 1967. Here are some of his requests:

I recommend the Truth-in-Lending Act of 1967. . . .

I recommend the Interstate Land Sales Full Disclosure Act of 1967. . . .

I recommend the Welfare and Pension Protection Act of 1967. . . .

I recommend the Medical Device Safety Act of 1967. . . .

I recommend the Clinical Laboratories Improvement Act of 1967. . . .

I recommend the Wholesome Meat Act of 1967. . . .

I recommend the Fire Safety Act of 1967. . . .

I recommend the Natural Gas Pipeline Safety Act of 1967. . . .

He also recommended that Congress give "careful consideration to the [346-page] report and recommendations of the Securities and Exchange Commission" on the detailed control of mutual funds, and that it enact new controls of the electric power industry as soon as a report by the Federal Power Commission was completed.

All this in one message. All this to be rushed through in 1967.

Furthermore, this message came when the most detailed regulation of special industries had already been enacted. On March 15, 1962, President Kennedy had sent a similar special message to Congress with similar recommendations. One result was that Congress that year passed a far more stringent drug-control law. Previously the government had power only to prevent the marketing of unsafe drugs. A new drug could be marketed if the government took no action within 60 days after an application was filed. The new law reversed this, and gave a bureaucrat power to hold up approval of a drug indefinitely until the manufacturer could prove to the bureaucrat's satisfaction that the drug was not only safe but "effective." This could give the bureaucrat life-or-death power over a company or its products. It is a very dubious legal principle that allows any bureaucrat to keep off the market something that, even though harmless, is in his opinion "ineffective," and that in addition puts the burden of proof of effectiveness on the producer. The new drug law has discouraged research and slowed down the introduction of new life-extending drugs.

Before President Johnson's 1967 message on consumer protection, an automobile safety law had been passed, as well as a food labelling and packaging law. Presumably the designs of future cars will not be specified by engineers, but by lawyers and congressmen, who will also take increasing control over labelling.

There is one very nasty by-product of this itch for more and more Federal control of business. The congressmen and bureaucrats who favor it begin by an enormous propaganda campaign against the industry or trade that they want to control. Thus, in order to get through the Wholesome Meat Act, government officials charged that unsafe and filthy meat was being sold almost everywhere. Then in order to get through a poultry-control bill, Miss Betty Furness, President Johnson's consumer adviser, stated: "There's not a place in the U. S. . . . where you can order a chicken sandwich with the confidence you are not endangering your health." Earlier in 1968, in a sweeping indictment, she had charged that every merchant was "after your back teeth."

A Senate committee recently held hearings to decide whether the automobile repair industry, with its tens of thousands of local garages and repairmen, ought not to be brought under direct Federal control. The committee credulously listened to witnesses who told it that the chances are 99 to 1 that work ordered will not be done properly, if it is done at all. The implication was left that the industry is made up mainly of incompetents and crooks.

Just how detailed were some of the new regulations that President Johnson was urging in his 1967 message can be judged from its passages on the control of medical devices. Government bureaucrats were to prescribe "standards" for "bone pins, catheters, X-ray equipment and diathermy machines." Bureaucrats were to say what kinds of nails and screws were to be used for bone repair, and what kinds of artificial eyes were to be permitted.

All this is an ominous reminder of medieval despotism. One thinks of the law of Henry VIII, which made it a penal offense to sell any pins but such as were "double-headed, and their head soldered fast to the shank, and well smoothed; and the shank well shaven; and the point well and round-filed and sharpened."

The pervading assumption of the Kennedy and Johnson Administrations was that any and all problems could be solved if only we piled up enough new laws and restrictions. Yet it may be doubted that consumers are going to be helped much by defaming and harassing producers.

The consumer has one great protection against incompetent producers or dishonest sellers. This is his own intelligence and his own decisions. His views are heard every day in his purchases and refusals to purchase. With every penny that he spends, the individual consumer is casting his vote for this product and against that. He does not need to sign petitions or march in picket lines. If he patronizes a product, the firm that makes it prospers and grows; if he stops buying a product, the firm that makes it goes out of business. The consumer is the boss. The producers must please him or die.

But this is another way of saying that the great protection of the consumer is the competition among producers for his patronage. This is another way of saying, as even President Johnson admitted in his consumer protection message, that: "Most of these problems are resolved in the free competitive market through the energies of private enterprise. It is remarkable how well the free enterprise system does its job." This was excellent lip service, but Mr. Johnson's detailed recommendations were based on the opposite assumption.

A thousand examples could be cited of the miraculous effect of free market competition in serving the consumer. I will content myself with one—the food industry.

The original packaging bill before the 89th Congress not only sought to protect the consumer against fraudulent or deceptive labelling and packaging, but it sought to standardize sizes, shapes and proportions of packages and net weights and quantities. Industry witnesses showed by numerous examples, however, how this would have discouraged innovation and restricted consumer choice. "If there are 8,000 different items in the average supermarket today as compared with 2,000 some years ago," testified Arthur E. Larkin, Jr., president of the General Foods Corporation, "it's because the consumer wants it that way. . . . No one of those 8,000 items will continue to be produced and occupy shelf space if the customers don't take it off the shelf and put it in their shopping bags. . . . Each product must win its right to survival. Each must be sold in sufficient quantity to be profitable."

In other words, once more, the way to protect the consumer is not to impede and harass, but to encourage the producer.

/\\./\\./\\./\\./\\.

CHAPTER 9

Famines Are Government-Made

/\\.

FOR THE LAST FEW YEARS AN INFLUENTIAL GROUP OF social reformers has been energetically propagating a dangerous myth. This is that the accelerating pace of population growth is overtaking the rate at which the world can produce food, and that disastrous famines are almost inevitable unless the growth of population can be throttled.

In October, 1966, a study by Prof. Karl Brandt, one of the world's great agricultural authorities, retired director of Stanford University's Food Research Institute and a former member of the President's Council of Economic Advisers, exploded this myth. But his analysis did not receive anything like the attention it deserved.

Governments' first priorities, Brandt declared, should not be to effect "planned parenthood crash programs," but to adopt policies that give farmers the freedom and incentive to expand food production.

Brandt has no quarrel with "planned parenthood by voluntary individual decision." But it would necessarily take years before even successful government birth control propaganda could appreciably affect the total size of the population. Moreover, the emphasis on birth control to counteract famine diverts attention from the enormous potential increase in food production that has now been made technically possible.

Science and technology have now developed overabundant sources of energy, which have opened the gates to replace human and animal power by mechanical power in food production.

The most crucial of all fertilizers, nitrogen, has now been made potentially abundant everywhere in the world at declining costs. One ton of pure nitrogen can yield from 15 to 20 tons of grain equivalent. Technology has developed new methods of irrigation, highly effective weed killers and pesticides, better means of storing and preserving perishables.

Why, then, has the world still been having famines? Brandt replies that in the last generation most of these famines have been primarily government-made. He cites the collectivist policies in Soviet Russia that initially resulted in the starvation of five million people and have continued to prevent any proper expansion of food output there for nearly forty years. Similar and worse policies have cost uncounted millions of lives in Red China.

Famine has been produced by similar policies in India. In its socialist mania for "industrialization," the Indian government has squeezed the major part of the capital for that industrialization out of farm income. It has arbitrarily set high prices for all manufactured goods and low prices for food and other farm products.

On top of this crushing discouragement to food production, mismanagement and neglect have led to a situation in which mice, rats, birds, and locusts are permitted to devour India's homegrown food faster than American Food for Peace can be shipped in at very high expense.

On top of all this, some 200 million government-protected sacred cows are allowed to roam around eating food while people are dying of hunger.

Our government has not insisted on any adequate conditions in return for our enormous gifts of food to India. So, Brandt concluded, our generosity has been contributing unwittingly to the prospect of real famine there, while weakening the United States dollar:

Such gifts allow the Indian government further leeway to continue ill-advised policies which suffocate the initiative of their farmers. The magnitude of food deficits these policies continue to create is so enormous that with all charity and foreign aid, we and the other industrial nations cannot possibly compensate for them.

/\.\/\.\/\.\/\.\/\.\

CHAPTER 10

Runaway Relief and Social Insecurity

/\.\

IN THE UNITED STATES, FEDERAL PROGRAMS TO RE-
lieve poverty and unemployment first went into effect
on a large scale in the Great Depression. The argument
was that they were needed only during the emergency.
Since then the nation has enjoyed a return of prosperity, an enormous growth in national income, a fall of
unemployment to record low levels, and a sharp decline
(by any consistent definition) in the number and proportion of the poor. Yet relief, unemployment insurance, Social Security, and scores of other welfare
programs have expanded at an accelerative rate.

In a 1935 message to Congress, President Franklin D.
Roosevelt declared: "The Federal Government must
and shall quit this business of relief . . . . Continued

dependence upon relief induces a spiritual and moral disintegration, fundamentally destructive to the national fiber."

The contention then made was that, if unemployment and old-age insurance programs were put into effect, poverty and distress would be relieved by contributory programs that did not destroy the incentives and self-respect of the recipients, and that relief could gradually be tapered off to negligible levels.

Let us look first at what has happened to Social Security itself. Since the original act of 1935 there have been constant additions and expansions of benefits. As early as 1939, both the benefit and tax provisions of the basic act were overhauled. The 1939 package added survivors' benefits.

In 1950, coverage was broadened substantially to include about 90 per cent of the employed labor force. (Initially it had been only about 60 per cent.) The length of working time required to qualify for coverage was sharply reduced.

In 1954 and 1956 there were further liberalizations of coverage. Disability benefits were added. The 1956 amendment dropped the minimum retirement age required for women from 65 to 62.

In 1958, benefits for dependents of disabled workers were added. In 1961 the retirement age for men was also reduced to 62, though with a lower level of benefits than was payable at 65.

The 1965 legislation added Medicare for some 20 million Americans over 65. It made a host of other expensive changes. To the traditional Social Security program it added a 7 per cent across-the-board increase in cash benefits to retired workers.

In addition to other changes, the scale of benefits was increased in 1952, 1954, 1958, and 1965.

The 1967 Social Security amendments increased pay-

ments to the 24 million beneficiaries by an average of
13 per cent, raised minimum benefits 25 per cent, increased benefits to non-insured persons over 72, and
also increased survivor and disability insurance benefits.

The original Social Security payroll tax was 1 per cent
of wages up to $3,000, to be paid both by workers and
employers. The combined rate of tax is now 9.6 per cent
of wages up to $7,800.

But nobody can seriously expect even these greatly
increased payroll taxes to pay for the liabilities that the
government has already undertaken. W. Rulon William-
son, the actuary for the Social Security Board from 1936
to 1947, estimated even before the latest increases that
it would take $150 billion more just to take care of those
who were already on the benefit rolls, and that it would
probably take at least $1 *trillion* to take care of the
families of those who are already paying Social Security
taxes, but have not yet retired. That estimate doesn't
cover Medicare.

What, meanwhile, has happened to the relief programs that unemployment insurance and Social
Security were designed to make unnecessary?

In 1937, the first full year in which the initial Federal
public assistance programs were in operation, $316 mil-
lion was paid out to relief clients under the federally
aided programs. In 1960 the comparable total had increased more than tenfold, to $3.3 billion.

Though the Federal contribution has been mounting
steadily during the years, the burden borne by the
States and localities has been mounting at an almost
equal rate. The amount of public aid alone paid out by
the States and localities increased from $624 million in
1935 to $3 billion in 1966. The total of all social welfare
expenditures borne by the States and localities alone
has grown from $3.3 billion in 1935 to $40.8 billion in

1966, and for 1968 was probably about $46 billion.

The Federal budget lists the total cost of "Federal Aid to the Poor" in 1960 at $9.5 billion. For 1969 the cost is listed at $27.7 billion, nearly three times as much.

These figures include the cost of aid to education, work and training, health, cash benefit payments, and other social welfare services. In the 1969 fiscal year, the Federal Government placed the number of persons on direct relief at 8.8 million. This was an increase of 60 per cent compared with the number twelve years before, though the rate of unemployment is lower than it was then.

The Federal Government estimated that there are still about 29 million "poor" by official definition (a family of four with an annual income under $3,335). Not only do the individual programs to "assist" them become more costly year by year, but new programs are constantly being added, though they overlap and duplicate each other. Upward of 70 agencies have been counted operating some 300 programs for uplifting people.

A detailed account of the waste and scandals that have accompanied these proliferating programs can be found in Shirley Scheibla's recent book, *Poverty Is Where the Money Is.**

In addition to specific antipoverty programs, the Federal Government's total welfare outlays—including agricultural subsidies, housing and community development, health, labor and welfare, education, and veterans' benefits—come to a staggering total for the single 1969 fiscal year of more than $68 billion.

Even so we have not finished yet. We must add the $46 billion annual welfare cost that falls on the States and localities, making a grand total of more than $114 billion.

*New Rochelle, N.Y.: Arlington House, 1968.

Yet nearly all the "reforms" that are being proposed, even under the new Republican Administration, are changes that would still further increase the Social Security and direct relief burden, not reduce it.

One of these proposals, which may even be enacted into law before this book appears, is that all welfare be placed in the hands of the Federal Government, with a uniform level of relief payments throughout the nation. The practical effect of this would be to reduce the present high relief payments in the big cities hardly at all, but to increase enormously the relief paid in the poorer States and in the country districts.

The relief recipients in the poorer States and country districts would not only, because of their comparatively much lower living costs, be much better off than the relief recipients in the big cities, but their relief payments would be so much higher in comparison with the local wage rates in their districts that hundreds of thousands more would prefer going on relief to staying at work.

As the relief system would probably be administered by the city and county governments, while the Federal taxpayers were footing the bill, all incentives to economy and the elimination of malingerers and chiselers from the relief rolls would fall to the vanishing point. The country would slide easily toward guaranteed-income plans, and the waste and corruption in relief payments would make present waste and corruption seem trivial in comparison.

/\./\./\./\./\

CHAPTER 11

Income Without Work

/\./\

A GROUP OF SOCIAL REFORMERS, IMPATIENT WITH the present "rag bag" of measures to combat poverty, proposes to wipe it out in a single swoop. The government would simply guarantee to everybody, regardless of whether or not he worked, could work, or was willing to work, a minimum income. This guaranteed income would be sufficient for his needs, "enough to enable him to live with dignity."

The reformers estimate that the guaranteed income ought to range somewhere between $3,000 and $6,000 a year for a family of four.

This is no longer merely the proposal of a few starry-eyed private individuals. The National Commission on Technology, Automation, and Economic Progress, es-

tablished by Congress in 1964, brought in a 115-page
report to the President on February 4, 1966, recom-
mending guaranteed incomes for all. And in January of
1966, the President's Council of Economic Advisers in-
dicated approval of "uniformly determined payments
to families based only on the amount by which their
incomes fall short of minimum subsistence levels." This
plan, they declared, "could be administered on a universal basis for all the poor and would be the most
direct approach to reducing poverty."

Since then an increasing number of endorsements of
the guaranteed income proposal (sometimes under the
euphemisms of "income maintenance" or "negative income tax") have come from private and official sources.
In June of 1968 a subcommittee of the Joint Economic
Committee of Congress held extensive hearings (which
ran in printed form to 720 pages) on "income maintenance programs." Though a Gallup Poll published at
the time showed 58 per cent of those questioned were
opposed outright to a guaranteed income, and only 36
per cent were in favor, the overwhelming majority of
the witnesses called by the committee favored some
form of guaranteed income.

The plan is spelled out and argued in detail in a book
called *The Guaranteed Income* (1966), a symposium of
articles by ten contributors, edited by Robert Theobald, who calls himself a "socio-economist." Mr. Theobald has contributed three of the articles, including his
preface.

Of the following three paragraphs, Mr. Theobald
prints the first two entirely in italics:

*This book proposes the establishment of new principles spe-
cifically designed to break the link between jobs and income.
Implementation of these principles must necessarily be carried out by the government . . . .*

We will need to adopt the concept of an absolute constitu-
tional right to an income. This would guarantee to every
citizen of the United States, and to every person who has
resided within the United States for a period of five consecu-
tive years, the right to an income from the Federal Govern-
ment to enable him to live with dignity. No government
agency, judicial body, or other organization whatsoever
should have the power to suspend or limit any payments
assured by these guarantees . . . .

If the right to these incomes should be withdrawn under
any circumstances, government would have the power to
deprive the individual not only of the pursuit of happiness,
but also of liberty and even, in effect, of life itself. This *abso-*
lute right to a due-income would be essentially a new principle of jurisprudence.

The contributors to this volume have arrived at these
extraordinary conclusions not only because they share
a number of strange ideas of jurisprudence, of "rights,"
of government, and of the true meaning of liberty and
tyranny, but because they share a number of major economic misconceptions.

Nearly all of them seem to share the belief, for example, that the growth of automation and "cybernation"
is eliminating jobs so fast (or soon will be) that there just
won't be jobs for even the most industrious. "The continuing impact of technical change will make it impossible to provide jobs for all who seek them." The goal of
"jobs for all" is "no longer valid." And so on.

Ancient Fears of Automation

The fears of permanent unemployment as a result of
technological progress are as old as the Industrial Revolution in the late eighteenth and early nineteenth centuries. They have been constantly reiterated in the last

35 to 40 years and as often completely refuted. It is sufficient to point out here that not only has the average unemployment of slightly less than 5 per cent in the last twenty years not been growing, and that two-thirds of the jobless have usually remained so for periods of not more than ten weeks, but that the total volume of *employment* in the United States has reached a new high record in nearly every one of these years.

Even if it were true, as the authors of the guaranteed income proposal contend, that the American free enterprise system will soon become so productive that more than anybody really wants can be produced in half the time it takes now, why would that mean the disappearance of jobs? And how could that justify half the population's, say, being forced to work forty hours a week to support the other half in complete idleness? Why couldn't everybody work only in the mornings? Or half in the mornings and the other half in the afternoons at the same machines? Or why could not some people come in on Mondays, others on Tuesdays, and so on? It is difficult to understand the logic or the sense of fairness of those who contend that as soon as there is less to be done some people must be supported in idleness by all the rest.

"An Absolute Right"

But that is precisely the contention of the advocates of the guaranteed annual income. These handout incomes are to be given as "an absolute constitutional right," and not to be withheld "under *any* circumstances" (Theobald's italics). This means that the recipients are to continue to get this income not only if they absolutely refuse to seek or take a job, but if they gam-

ble the handout money away at the races or spend it on
prostitutes, pornography, whiskey, cigarettes, mari-
juana, heroin, or whatnot. They are to be given "sufficient to live in dignity," and it is apparently to be no
business of the taxpayers if a recipient chooses
nonetheless to live *without* dignity, and to devote his
guaranteed leisure to gambling, dissipation, drunken-
ness, debauchery, dope addiction, or even a life of
crime. "No government agency, judicial body, or other
organization whatsoever should have the power to suspend or limit any payments assured by these guarantees." This is surely a "new principle of jurisprudence."

Unrealistic Cost Estimates

How much income do the guaranteed-income advocates propose to guarantee? They differ regarding this,
but practically all of them think the government should
guarantee at least what they and government officials
call the "minimum maintenance level" or the "poverty-
income line." The Social Security Administration calculated that the 1964 poverty-income line for non-farm
individuals was $1,540 a year. A non-farm family of four
was defined as poor if its money income was below
$3,130. The Council of Economic Advisers calculated
that by this standard 34 million, or 18 per cent, of our
190 million 1964 population were living in poverty. This
is in spite of the $40 billion total spent in welfare pay-
ments, of which it estimated that $20 billion (in the
fiscal year 1965) went to persons who were, or would
otherwise have been, below the poverty-income line.

The official "poverty-income line" is constantly rising, and in spite of the smaller number of persons officially estimated to be poor, Federal payments to them

have been rising even faster. According to President Johnson's annual budget message of January 29, 1968, "there remain about 29 million poor. In fiscal year 1969, Federal outlays which aid persons below the poverty line (for example, a family of four with an annual income under $3,335) are estimated to total $27.7 billion. This represents an increase of $3.1 billion over fiscal year 1968 and $15.2 billion over 1963."

How much would a guaranteed-income program cost the taxpayers? This would depend, of course, on how big an income was being guaranteed. Many of the income-guarantee advocates think that a guarantee merely of the poverty-line income would be totally inadequate. They appeal to other "minimum" budgets put together by the Social Security Administration or the Bureau of Labor Statistics, some of which run up to nearly $6,000 for a family of four.

One of the contributors to the Theobald symposium makes the following estimates of the cost to the taxpayers of different guarantees:

For a "minimum maintenance" level of $3,000 a year: total cost, $11 billion a year.

For an "economy" level of $4,000: $23 billion a year.

For a "modest-but-adequate" level of $5,000: $38 billion a year.

These figures are huge, yet they are clearly an underestimate. For the calculations take it for granted that those who could get government checks to bring their incomes to $3,000 or $5,000 a year, as an absolute guarantee, without conditions, would continue to go on earning just as much as before. But, as even one of the contributors to the Theobald symposium, William Vogt, remarked: "Those who believe that men will want to work whether they have to or not seem to have lived sheltered lives."

Who Would Do the Work?

Vogt goes on to point out, with refreshing realism,
how hard it is even today, before any guaranteed income, to get people to shine shoes, wash cars, cut brush,
mow lawns, act as porters at railroad or bus stations, or
do any number of other necessary jobs. "Millions of
service jobs are unfilled in the United States, and it is
obvious that men and women will often prefer to exist
on small welfare payments rather than take the jobs. . . .
If this situation exists before the guaranteed income is
made available, who is going to take care of services
when everyone can live without working—as a right?"

Who is, in fact, going to take the smelly jobs, or any
low-paid job, once the guaranteed income program is in
effect? Suppose, as a married man with two children,
your present income from some nasty and irregular
work is $2,500 a year. Comes the income guarantee, and
you get a check in the mail from the government for
$900. This is accompanied by a letter telling you that
you are entitled as a matter of unconditional right to the
poverty-line income of $3,400, and this $900 is for the
difference between that and your earned income of
$2,500. You are happy—for just a day. Then it occurs to
you that you are a fool to go on working at your nasty
job or series of odd jobs for $2,500 when you can stop
work entirely and get the full $3,400 from the govern-
ment.

So the government would, in fact, have to pay out a
tremendous sum. In addition, the program would create
idleness on a huge scale. To predict this result is not to
take a cynical view, but merely to recognize realities.
The beneficiaries of the guaranteed income would
merely be acting sensibly from their own point of view.
But the result would be that the more than one-seventh
of the population now judged to be below the poverty

line would stop producing even most of the necessary goods and services it is producing now. The unpleasant jobs would not get done. There would be less total production, or total real income, to be shared by everybody.

The Shifting "Poverty Line"

But so far we have been talking about the effect of the guaranteed income on the recipients whose previous incomes have been below the poverty line. What about the other six-sevenths of the population, whose incomes have been above it? What would be the effect on *their* incentives and actions?

Suppose a married man with two children found at the end of a year that he had earned $3,500? And suppose he found that his neighbor, with the same-sized family, had simply watched television, hung around a bar, or gone fishing during the year and had got a guaranteed income from the government of $3,400? Wouldn't the worker begin to think that he had been something of a sap to work so hard for a mere $100 net, and that it would be much better to lead a pleasantly idle life for just that much less? And wouldn't the same thing occur to all others whose earned incomes were only slightly above the guarantee?

It is not easy to say how far above the guarantee any man's income would have to be for this consideration not to occur to him. But we would do well to remember the following figures: The *median* or "middle" income for all families in 1966 was $7,436. The median income for "unrelated" individuals was $2,270. People with these incomes or less, i.e., half the population, would be near enough to the guarantee to wonder why they weren't getting any of it.

Someone Must Pay

If "*everybody* should receive a guaranteed income as
a matter of right" (and the italics are Mr. Theobald's),
who is to pay him that income? The advocates of the
guaranteed income gloss over this problem. The money,
they tell us, will be paid by the "government" or by the
"State." "The State would acknowledge the duty to
maintain the individual."

The State is a shadowy entity that apparently gets its
money out of some fourth dimension. The truth is, of
course, that the government has nothing to give to anybody that it doesn't first take from someone else. The
whole guaranteed-income proposal is a perfect modern
example of the shrewd observation of the French
economist, Bastiat, more than a century ago: "The State
is the great fiction by which everybody tries to live at
the expense of everybody else."

Rights vs. Obligations

None of the guaranteed-income advocates explicitly
recognizes that real "income" is not paper money that
can be printed at will, but goods and services, and that
somebody has to produce these goods and services by
hard work. The proposition of the guaranteed-income
advocates, in plain words, is that the people who work
must be taxed to support not only the people who can't
work but the people who won't work. The workers are
to be forced to give up part of the goods and services
they have created and turn them over to the people
who haven't created them or flatly refuse to create
them.

Once this proposition is stated bluntly, the spurious-
ness in all the rhetoric about "the absolute constitu-

tional 'right' to an income" becomes clear. A true legal
or moral right of one man always implies an *obligation*
on the part of others to do something or refrain from
doing something to ensure that right. If a creditor has
a right to a sum of money owed to him on a certain day,
the debtor has an obligation to pay it. If I have a right
to freedom of speech, to privacy, or to the ownership
of a house, everyone else has an obligation to respect it.
But when Paul claims a "right" to "an income sufficient
to live in dignity," whether he is willing to work for it
or not, what he is really claiming is a right to part of
somebody else's earned income. What Paul is asserting
is that Peter has a duty to earn more than he needs or
wants to live on so that the surplus may be seized from
him and turned over to Paul to live on.

What the guaranteed-income advocates are really
saying, behind all their high-sounding phrases and
humanitarian rhetoric, is something like this: "Look, we
find ourselves with this wonderful apparatus of coercion, the government and its police forces. Why not use
it to force the workers to pay part of their earnings over
to the non-workers?"

Lack of Understanding

We can still believe in the sincerity and good inten-
tions of these people, but only by assuming an appalling
lack of understanding on their part of the most elementary economic principles. "This book," writes Robert
Theobald, "proposes the establishment of new principles specifically designed to break the link between
jobs and income." But we cannot break the link between jobs and income. True income is not money, but
the goods and services that money will buy. These
goods and services have to be produced. They can only

be produced by work, by jobs. We may, of course, break
the link between the job and the income *of a particular
person,* say Paul, by giving him an income whether he
consents to take a job or not. But we can do this only by
seizing part of the income of some other person, say
Peter, from *his* job. To believe we can break the link
between jobs and income is to believe we can break the
link between production and consumption. Goods have
to be produced by somebody before they can be con-
sumed by anybody.

Claimants to Be Trusted, Taxpayers to Be Examined

One reason for the agitation for an unconditionally
guaranteed income is the dislike of some social reformers for the "means test." The means test is disliked on
two grounds: that it is "humiliating" or "degrading,"
and that it is administratively troublesome—"a comprehensive examination of means and resources, applicant
by applicant." The guaranteed-income advocates think
they can do away with all this by using the "simple"
mechanism of having everybody fill out an income tax
blank, whereupon the government would send a check
to everybody for the amount that his income, so reported, fell below the government's set "poverty-line"
minimum.

The belief that this income tax mechanism would be
administratively simple is a delusion. Before the introduction of the withholding mechanism, before the reporting requirements for payments made to individuals
in excess of $600 in any year, and the still more recent
requirements for the reporting of even the smallest interest and dividend payments, the income tax was in
large part a self-imposed tax. The government de-
pended heavily on the taxpayer's conscientiousness

and honesty. To a substantial extent it still does.

The government can check the honesty of individual returns only by a random or arbitrary sampling process. It is altogether probable that more evasion and cheating go on in the low income tax returns than in the high ones—not because the big-income earners are more honest, but simply because their chances of being examined and caught are higher. The amount of concealment and falsification that would be practiced by persons trying to get as high a guaranteed income as possible would probably be enormous. To minimize the swindling the government would have to resort to the same case-by-case and applicant-by-applicant process as it does to administer current relief, unemployment insurance, and Social Security programs.

Is a means test for relief necessarily any more humiliating than the ordeal that the taxpayer must go through when his income tax is being examined—when every question he is asked and record he is required to provide implies that he is a potential crook? If the reply is that this inquisition is necessary to protect the government from fraud, then the same reply is valid as applied to applicants for relief or a guaranteed income. It would be a strange double standard to insist that those who were being forced to pay the guaranteed income to others should be subject to an investigation from which those who applied for the guaranteed income would be exempt.

In short, to prevent the worst scandals and injustices, even by the standards of the guaranteed income's advocates, some test of need would be inescapable. If we fixed things so that there was no loss of dignity or self-respect whatever in being idle and taking a handout, then there would be no gain in dignity or self-respect in working and earning one's own living. It goes without saying that any need test or means test should be

administered without any *unnecessary* infringement of
the privacy or dignity of the person or family concerned, but such a test would still have to be at least as
careful and thorough as a typical income tax examination.

Comparison with the income tax may also remind us
of some of the real complications that the guaranteed-
income and "negative-income-tax" proposals gloss
over. Some of these complications were almost acciden-
tally brought out by Dr. Joseph A. Pechman, director of
economic studies for the Brookings Institution, in his
testimony of June 13, 1968, before a subcommittee of
the Congressional Joint Economic Committee. It is important to keep in mind that Dr. Pechman was testify-
ing in *favor* of the guaranteed income, but was
earnestly considering some of the "anomalous situa-
tions" that might arise under it.

"For example," he pointed out, "an individual own-
ing $100,000 worth of IBM stock receives cash divi-
dends of less than $1,000 annually." Should such a
person, if this were his only income, receive, say a $2,-
400 a year annual handout to bring his family's income
up to the $3,400 poverty-line level? Even Dr. Pechman
was inclined to think not. But he did apparently think
that an individual who received only $1,000 from not
more than $25,000 worth of bonds or stock (or other
assets of the same market worth) should get this supplementary income.

Most of us, I think, would question this judgment.
Among the dissenters, I am confident, would be the
man who had received only $1,000, but entirely in
wages, and the man who had received $3,401 during the
year, also entirely in wages—neither of them with any
capital assets to speak of, and certainly not a nest egg
of $25,000.

But this is only one of a score of major difficulties

raised by the simplistic proposal for a guaranteed income. The income tax mechanism would be irrelevant to the real problem with which the guaranteed-income advocates profess to be concerned. For the applicants would presumably be reporting *last* year's income, which would have no necessary relation to their present need. An applicant's income in the previous year or other previous period might be much higher or much lower than it is today. The process would not meet present emergencies, such as illness or temporary loss of employment. The guaranteed-income payment might either come too late or prove unneeded or excessive.

When such difficulties are pointed out to them, the guaranteed-income champions quickly improvise amendments. Revised income estimates for the current year might be made quarterly, say. But to meet the cash needs of the officially designated poor, the government's payments would have to be made monthly or even weekly, and in the month or week in which the actual need existed, not later. The guaranteed-incomers have now started to talk of monthly revisions of income estimates, of payments of arrears, of reimbursements to the government for overpayments, etc. Putting aside the question of how realistic it is to talk of getting 30 million poor to return overpayments made to them, we have only to think of the administrative nightmare of payment adjustments, examinations, verifications, and so on, of this "simple" income tax plan.

The Insistence on Cash

A word needs to be said at this point, also, about the insistence of the guaranteed-income advocates that the government make its relief payments in *cash*. They rest this insistence on a spurious libertarian argument. The only trouble with the poor, they smilingly argue, is lack of money. We should therefore give them this money, and not attempt to dictate how and on what they should spend it (let alone give them relief in kind), because we should not interfere with their liberty to spend their government cash but "let them make their own mistakes."

The trouble with this argument is that it is precisely because so many of the poor have shown an incapacity for knowing how to spend as well as how to earn money that they suffer as many of the pangs of poverty as they do. Cash is the very last thing to be given to a compulsive gambler, a drunkard, or a drug addict. As soon as he has gambled the money away, or spent it on whiskey or heroin, is the government to telegraph him more? But if it doesn't, how is it to see that he and his family get proper nourishment, or that he has enough left over for the rent, or that his family are decently dressed, or that his children are properly educated? This is the kind of central problem that must arise if all the poor are to be indiscriminately handed cash incomes, not only regardless of whether they are willing to work or not, but of whether or not they show any responsibility or common sense in what they spend the money on.

I recently found an encouraging sign that a turn of thought may be coming on this subject, at least in England, and that some people may begin to recognize that our forefathers' policies with regard to relief were not the result merely of blindness and cruelty. In its leading editorial of September 7, 1968, the London *Daily Telegraph* wrote:

The trouble is that if the poorest are too well cared for by cash handouts from the State they may never have any incentive to get their feet on the next rung of the economic ladder. So why not give them, say, food, fuel, and clothes for their children in kind rather than everything in cash? There would then be the assurance that the help was being properly directed. And if the recipients were not well pleased with such paternalism, they would have the incentive to work instead. Some such radical rethinking is long overdue.

Let me add that the argument that we must respect the liberty of the poor by giving them handouts solely in cash is spurious from still another standpoint. It overlooks the liberties of the industrious and prudent people from whom money is being either withheld or seized, in order to pay the cash handouts. It makes no sense to preserve the "liberty" of the irresponsible at the expense of the liberty of the responsible.

Old Subsidies Never Die

One of the main selling arguments of the guaranteed-income advocates is that its net cost to the taxpayers would not be as great as might appear at first sight because it would be a *substitute* for the present "mosaic" or "rag bag" of measures designed to meet the same goal—Social Security, unemployment compensation, Medicare, direct relief, free school lunches, food stamp plans, farm subsidies, housing subsidies, rent subsidies, and all the rest.

Neither the record of the past nor a knowledge of political realities supports such an expectation. One of the main selling arguments in the middle Nineteen Thirties, first for unemployment insurance and later for Social Security, was that these programs would take the place of and eliminate the need for the various relief programs and payments then in existence. But in the last thirty years these programs have continued to grow year by year with only minor interruptions.

Let me remind the reader of some of the comparisons of welfare expenditures in the preceding chapter. In spite of the Federal Social Security program, the amount of public aid alone paid out by the States and localities has grown from $3.3 billion in 1935 to about $46 billion in 1968. The Federal Government estimated the number of people on direct relief in the fiscal year 1969 at 8.8 million, or 60 per cent more than the number twelve years ago. "Federal Aid to the Poor" tripled in nine years from $9.5 billion in 1960 to $27.7 billion in fiscal 1969. And when we throw in Social Security and all the rest, the total annual welfare costs that fall on the Federal Government, States and localities combined come to the staggering total for fiscal 1969 of more than $114 billion.

So we may expect not only that the guaranteed income would be thrown on top of all existing welfare payments (we can expect a tremendous outcry, plus demonstrations and riots, against discontinuing any of them), but that demands would arise for constant enlargement of the guaranteed amount. If the average payment were merely the *difference* between an assumed "poverty-line" income of, say, $3,400 and what the family had earned itself, all heads of families earning less than $3,400 would either quit work or threaten to do so unless they were given the full $3,400, and allowed to "keep" whatever they earned themselves. And once this demand was granted (in an effort to avoid the wholesale idleness and pauperization that would otherwise occur), the people whose earnings were just above the government minimum, or less than twice as much, would point out how unjustly they were being treated. And the only "logical" and "fair" stopping place, it would be argued, would be to give *everybody* the full minimum of $3,400 no matter how much he was earning or getting from other sources.

Anyone who thinks such a prediction far-fetched need merely recall how we got into the present system of paying everybody over 72 Social Security benefits regardless of his current earnings from other sources, and paying benefits to every retired person over 65 regardless of the size of his unearned income from other sources. By the same logic, the British government pays comprehensive unemployment, sickness, maternity, widowhood, funeral and other benefits, and retirement pensions, regardless of need or the size of the recipient's income. The demand for universal "childrens' allowances" or "family allowances" is also based on this logic.

Incentive Undermined

I should like to return here to the question of incentives. I have already pointed out how the guaranteed-income plan, if adopted in the form that its advocates propose, would lead to wholesale idleness and pauperization among nearly all those earning less than the minimum guarantee, and among many earning just a little more. But in addition to the erosion of the incentive to work, there would be just as serious an erosion of the incentive to save. The main reason most people save is to meet possible but unforeseeable contingencies, such as illness, accidents, or the loss of a job. If everyone were guaranteed a minimum cash income by the government, this main incentive for saving would disappear. The important habit of saving might disappear with it.

The more affluent minority, it is true, also save toward a retirement income in old age or for supplementary income in their working years. But with the prevalence of a guaranteed-income system, this type of saving also would be profoundly discouraged. This would be certain to mean a reduction in both the nation's capital accumulation and the investment in more and new and better tools, plants and equipment upon which all of us depend for increased national productivity, increased real wages, more lucrative employment, and economic progress in general. We might even enter an era of net capital consumption. In other words, the long-term effect of a guaranteed-income plan would be to increase poverty, not to reduce it.

It is important to point out that to be concerned with the destructive effects of a guaranteed-income program on the incentives of people to work and save, is not to pass a wholesale moral judgment on the present poor. We must avoid on the one hand the sweeping assumption, sometimes made by conservatives, that the poor have no one to blame for their poverty but themselves, and yet resist on the other hand the frequent sweeping "liberal" assumption that all the poor or jobless are poor or jobless "through no fault of their own." The only realistic presumption is that *some* people are poor or jobless through no fault of their own, that some are poor or jobless entirely through fault of their own, but that the great majority are poor or jobless through various complicated mixtures of misfortune and personal mistakes or shortcomings.

These mixtures differ in each case, ranging from those in which misfortune predominates to those in which personal shortcomings predominate. If we must simplify, we come back to the old Victorian distinction between the "deserving" and the "undeserving" poor. People today are justifiably reluctant to state the distinction in moral terms. Nevertheless, the distinction between those who are trying to cure their poverty by their own efforts, and those who are not, is vital for any workable solution of the problem of poverty. The central vice is that they ignore this distinction. The result of all the guaranteed-income and "negative income tax" schemes is that these schemes would destroy incentives on a wholesale scale, and therefore have the opposite of their intended effect.

It is not merely the effect of guaranteed-income proposals in undermining the incentives of those earning less than the guarantee that we need to be concerned about, but the effect of such proposals in undermining the incentives of those much further up in the income scale. For they would not only be deprived of the benefits that they saw millions of others getting. It is *they* who would be expected to *pay* these benefits, through the imposition upon them of far more burdensome income taxes than they were already paying. If these taxes were steeply progressive in proportion to income, as is probable, they would discourage long hours and unusual effort.

It is difficult to make any precise estimate of the effect of a given income tax rate in discouraging or reducing work and production. Different individuals will, of course, be differently affected. The activities of a man whose whole income comes in the form of a single salary from a single job will be differently affected than those of a surgeon, a doctor, a writer, an actor, an architect, or anyone whose income varies with the number of assignments he is willing to undertake or clients he is willing to serve.

What we do know is that the higher income tax rates, contrary to popular belief, just don't raise revenue. In the 1969 fiscal year, individual income taxes were estimated to be raising $81 billion (out of total revenues of $136 billion). Yet the tax rates in excess of 50 per cent have been bringing in less than $400 million a year— less than 1 per cent of total income tax revenues and not enough to run even the present government for a full day. (In other words, if all the personal income tax rates above 50 per cent were reduced to that level, the loss in revenue would be less than about $400 million.) If these rates above 50 per cent were raised further, it is more probable that they would raise less revenue than more. Therefore, it is the income tax rates on the lower and middle incomes that would have to be raised most, for the simple reason that 80 per cent of the personal income of the country is earned by people with less than $20,000 gross incomes.

Poverty for All

It is certain that high income tax rates discourage and reduce the earning of income, and therefore the total production of wealth, to some extent. Suppose, for illustration, we begin with the extreme proposal that we equalize everybody's income by taxing away all income in excess of the average in order to pay it over to those with incomes below the average. (The guaranteed-income proposal isn't too far away from that!)

Let us say that the present per capita average yearly income in the United States is about $3,000. Then everybody who was getting less than that (and would get just that whether he worked or not) would, of course, as with the guaranteed-income proposal, not need to work productively at all. And no one who was earning more than $3,000 would find it worth while to continue to earn the excess, because it would be seized from him in any case. More, it would soon occur to him that it wasn't worthwhile earning even the $3,000, for it would be given to him in any case; and his income would be the same, whether he worked or not. So if everybody acted under an income equalization program merely in the way that seemed most rational in his own interest considered in isolation, none of us would work and all of us would starve. We might each get $3,000 cash (if someone could be found to continue to run the printing machines just for the fun of it), but there would be nothing to buy with it.

A less extreme equalization program would, of course, have less extreme results. If only 90 per cent of all incomes over $3,000 were seized and people could keep 10 cents of every "excess" dollar they earned, there would of course still be a tiny incentive to earn a little more. And if everyone could keep 25 cents out of every dollar he earned above the $3,000, the incentive would be slightly higher.

But every tax or expropriation must reduce incentives to a certain extent. The effect of the guaranteed-income proposal would be practically to wipe out incentives for those earning (or even wanting) no more than the guarantee, and greatly to reduce incentives for all those earning or capable of earning more than the guarantee. Therefore the guaranteed income would reduce effort and earning and production. It would violently reduce the national income (measured in real terms). And it would reduce the standard of living for the taxpaying five-sixths of the population. The government might be able to pay out the specified amount of guaranteed *dollar* "income," but the purchasing power of the dollars would appallingly shrink.

/\/\/\/\/\

CHAPTER 12

Fallacies of the Negative Income Tax

/\

RECOGNIZING THE CALAMITOUS EROSION OF INCEN-
tives that would be brought about by a straight guaranteed-income plan, other reformers have advocated
what they call a "negative income tax." This proposal
was put forward by the prominent economist, Professor
Milton Friedman, of the University of Chicago, in his
book *Capitalism and Freedom,* which appeared in 1962.
The system he proposed would be administered along
with the current income tax system.

Suppose that the poverty-line income were set at $3,-
000 per "consumer unit" (families or individuals), and
suppose that the negative income tax (which is really a
subsidy), were a flat rate of 50 per cent. Then every
"consumer unit" (this is the statisticians' technical

term) whose income fell below $3,000 would be paid a subsidy of, say, 50 per cent of the difference. If its earned income were $2,000, for example, it would receive $500; if its earned income were $1,000 it would receive $1,000; if its earned income were zero it would receive $1,500.

Professor Friedman freely concedes that his proposal, "like any other measure to relieve poverty... reduces the incentives of those helped to help themselves." But he argues that "it does not eliminate that incentive entirely, as a system of supplementing incomes up to some fixed minimum would. An extra dollar earned always means more money available for expenditure."

It is true that a "negative income tax"* (which is a misleading name for a tapered-off guaranteed income) would not have quite as destructive an effect on incentives as would a straight guaranteed income. In fact, some thirty years ago I put forward a similar proposal myself. This appeared in an article in *The Annalist* (a weekly then published by the New York *Times*) of January 4, 1939. I suggested what I called a "tapering subsidy," a relief payment that would be reduced by only $1 for every $2 the relief recipient earned by himself. But I abandoned the proposal when I realized that it leads straight into a dilemma, which is precisely the dilemma of the negative income tax: Either it is altogether inadequate at the lower end of the scale of self-earnings, or it is unjustifiably excessive at the higher end. Either it must pay only half an adequate income (by its own definition of "adequate") to a family that earns no income, or it must pay nearly twice an adequate income to a family that already earns an almost adequate income.

---

*Trick names of this sort corrupt the language and confuse thought. It would hardly clarify matters to call a handout a "negative deprivation" or having your pocket picked "receiving a negative gift."

The problem that the NIT (negative income tax) evades or glosses over is the problem of the individual or family with zero income. If an individual were given only $300 (the figure suggested in Professor Friedman's original proposal in 1962), nobody would regard this as nearly adequate—particularly if, as Professor Friedman also proposed, NIT were made a complete substitute for all other forms of relief and welfare. If the NIT payment for a family of zero income is set at $1,700, no advocate of the guaranteed income would regard it as adequate to live on in "decency and dignity." So if the NIT were ever adopted, the political pressure would be irrestible to make it provide the minimum "poverty-line" income of $3,400 even to families with zero earned income.

The basic subsidy would therefore be as great as under the straight guaranteed income. But if the basic subsidy under NIT to a family with zero income were $3,400, then under the NIT 50 per cent "incentive" formula that family would continue to get some government subsidy until its annual income reached $6,800. But this is higher than the median family income for the whole country in 1963 ($6,637). In brief, this would be fantastically expensive.

In addition, it would raise serious problems of equity. When the subsidized family was earning $6,798 income it would still be getting a $1 subsidy. When it earned $6,802 would it fall off the gravy train entirely, and have to wait until its income fell below $3,400 before it could get on again? And what about the family that had been earning $3,402 all along, and had never got on the gravy train?

The arithmetical dilemma of the NIT has received so little attention from its advocates that I hope I may be forgiven another illustration to show the paradoxical way in which it would work out.

An orthodox relief program would pay the jobless head of a family, say, $60 a week. If he then started to earn something, he would be paid simply the *difference* between that amount and $60. Under the NIT principle a man who was earning nothing would also receive a relief payment of $60 a week. But if he then earned $30 a week on his own he would still get a $45 payment (reduced by only $1 for every $2 earnings), bringing his total income to $75 a week. If he was later able to earn the full $60 for himself he would still be getting a relief payment of $30 a week, bringing his total income to $90. In fact, even if he succeeded in bringing his total self-earnings to $118 a week he would still be getting $1 a week in relief payment.

He would then be almost twice as well off economically as he would if he had always earned enough—say, $61 a week—not to get on the relief rolls in the first place. This would be clearly inequitable to those who had never got on relief. The incentive to get on relief, and certainly to stay on relief, would be enormously greater under NIT than under the present system.

If we tried to escape this result by using the NIT formula only in part—taking the man off relief, say, as soon as he was himself earning $60 a week—we would get an even more absurd result. When he was earning $58 a week under NIT, he would still be getting $31 a week from the government, making his total income $89. But if he then made the mistake of earning only $2 more he would end up with a net *loss* of $29 a week. So the negative income tax would create a tremendous positive incentive to get and stay on relief permanently.

The NIT scheme could avoid this preposterous result by paying a man with zero income only, say, $30 a week, or only half as much as its own proponents assume that he needs to live on.

Some readers may think that the dilemma of the NIT

88 MAN vs. THE WELFARE STATE

scheme can somehow be escaped by changing the percentage by which the relief payment or income supplement is reduced as self-earnings increase. But any
change from 50 per cent one way or the other merely
reduces one horn of the dilemma by making the other
more formidable. If we reduce the government supplement by 75 cents for every dollar of self-earnings, we
correspondingly reduce or destroy the incentive for
such self-earnings. If we reduce the government supplement by only 25 cents for every dollar of self-earnings, we increase the recipient's incentive to work and
earn, but at the cost of a still more expensive program
for the government, and we increase the recipient's
positive incentive to stay on relief because of the violent drop in his income if he ever got off. If we make the
scheme more complicated by, say, reducing the relief
payment or supplementary income by only 25 cents for
every dollar of the recipient's first $10 of weekly self-
earnings, 50 cents for every dollar of his second $10 of
self-earnings, and 75 cents for every dollar of his third
$10 of self-earnings, or some similar scheme, we merely
pile up an administrative nightmare without solving the
basic dilemma. The unpalatable truth seems to be that
whenever we try to "increase incentives" by reducing
a relief payment by less than a dollar for every additional dollar of self-earnings, we solve an immediate
problem at the cost of building up a bigger problem for
the future.

In addition to the special dilemma it presents, the
NIT retains the fatal defects of the straight guaranteed
income. By neglecting the careful applicant-by-applicant investigation of needs and resources made by the
ordinary relief system, it would open the government to
massive fraud, chiseling, and swindling. And it would
also, like the guaranteed income, force the taxpayers to
support a man regardless of whether or not he was

making any sincere effort to support himself. The government is bound to get into insoluble difficulties if it starts to give money away to "the poor" not only without making sure that they are poor but without bothering to find out the reasons why any particular individual or family is poor.

How Much Would It Cost?

How much would a guaranteed-income or NIT program cost? I have already pointed out that proponents have put out calculations as high as $38 billion a year, but we may be confident that their cost figures are systematically underestimated, even for the early years. And if once the main principle of either proposal were accepted, the minimum subsidy or guarantee demanded would be bound constantly to increase. Anyone who doubts this need merely consult the history of unemployment insurance and Social Security benefits since those plans were initiated in the Nineteen Thirties. (They too were going to replace straight relief, which, however, continues to grow at an alarming pace.)

Is there any assurance that a guaranteed-income or NIT plan would not also grow as rapidly? Present indications are that it might grow even faster. It is significant, as I have pointed out previously, that when Professor Milton Friedman first proposed his NIT plan in 1962, in his *Capitalism and Freedom,* he was suggesting that an individual with zero income receive a subsidy of the modest amount of $300. Now he is talking mainly in terms of a family of four and suggests that such a family, with no other income, should receive a basic amount from the government of $1,500. But already there is a prominent competitive scheme (pub-

lished by the Brookings Institution, and written by Dr.
James Tobin of Yale, Dr. Joseph A. Pechman, the Brookings Institution's director of economic studies, and Dr.
Peter M. Mieszkowski) that offers much more generous
subsidies. Once the scheme gets into practical politics,
we can expect the competitive bidding to get going in
earnest.

So knowing what we do of political pressures, and of
the past history of relief, "social insurance," and other
"antipoverty" measures, we are forced to conclude that
once the principle of either the NIT or the straight
guaranteed income were accepted, it would be made
an addition to and not a substitute for the present con-
glomeration of relief and "antipoverty" programs. And
even alone it would drastically reduce the productive
incentives of those earning less than the guaranteed
amount and seriously reduce the incentives of those
earning more, because of the oppressive taxation it
would necessarily involve. Its overall effect would be to
level real incomes down, not up.

Let us take a closer look at the problem of raising
taxation still further to pay for a guaranteed-income or
NIT program. It is obvious that we could not expect
such a program to be paid for merely by the very rich.
If we were to subsidize all family incomes below $3,400
(let alone $6,800), it would hardly be consistent to tax
them. Yet even before the income tax increase of 1968,
single persons with *net* incomes (after exemptions and
deductions) of $500 paid 14 per cent on such income, 15
per cent on the next $500, and so on, so that persons
with net incomes below $6,000 were taxed at rates up
to 22 per cent.

In 1965, moreover, taxpayers with adjusted gross incomes under $15,000 (who received more than three-
quarters of the total personal income there was to be
taxed) paid 61.5 per cent of the entire personal income

tax. Taxpayers with adjusted gross incomes under $20,000 paid 70 per cent of the entire personal income tax.

Why not collect the major part of the income tax, someone may ask, from the really big incomes? Because taxpayers with adjusted gross incomes above $50,000 received even before taxes only 5 per cent of the nation's adjusted gross incomes.

So when advocates of the guaranteed income and similar schemes insist self-righteously that "we can afford" to pay for more and more of such schemes, they ought to specify just who "we" are. They ought to explain to people who are earning their incomes the hard way why they really don't need all that they bother to earn for their own families, and tell them also just how much more they can "afford" to have taken away from them.

Neither a "negative income tax" nor a guaranteed-income plan of the dimensions now being suggested could possibly be put into effect with dollars of present purchasing power.

The Poor Laws of England

Even at present our large and overlapping assortment of relief and antipoverty measures is seriously reducing incentives to the production that would otherwise be possible. Our social reformers have been everywhere overlooking the two-sided nature of the problem of reducing poverty. The obstinate two-sided problem we face is this: *How can we mitigate the penalties of misfortune and failure without undermining the incentives to effort and success?*

Our social reformers—who sometimes talk as if no government ever did anything to relieve the plight of the jobless and the poor until the New Deal came along in 1933—are constantly deploring the alleged indifference, callousness, or niggardliness of our forefathers in dealing with the poor. But wholly apart from private charity, previous generations in their governmental capacity were sharply aware of the problem of poverty and made some effort to alleviate it almost as far back as the records go. There were "poor laws" in England even before the days of Queen Elizabeth. A statute of 1536 provided for the collection of voluntary funds for the relief of those unable to work. Eleven years later the City of London decided that these voluntary collections were insufficient, and imposed a compulsory tax to support the poor. In 1572 a compulsory tax for this purpose was imposed on a national scale.

But the problem soon proved a very serious one for the people of that age. The upper class was very small numerically and proportionately. The middle class itself was always very close to what we would call the poverty line. The workhouse and other conditions imposed on those on relief seem very cruel to us today. But our ancestors were in constant fear that if they increased relief or relaxed the stern conditions for it they would pauperize increasing numbers of the population and create an insoluble problem.

At the beginning of the nineteenth century, indeed, the cost of poor relief began to get out of hand. The total cost of the poor law administration increased fourfold in the thirty-two years between 1785 and 1817, and reached a sixth of the total public expenditure. One Buckinghamshire village reported in 1832 that its expenditure on poor relief was eight times what it had been in 1795, and more than the rental of the whole parish had been in that year.

In face of statistics of this kind, England's Whig government decided to intervene. It appointed a royal commission, and in 1834 a new and more severe poor law was passed in accordance with the commission's recommendations.

The guiding principle of the new law was that poor relief should be granted to able-bodied poor and their dependents only in well-regulated workhouses under conditions inferior to those of the humblest laborers outside. This seemed harsh, but the commissioners had argued that "every penny bestowed that tends to render the condition of the pauper more eligible than that of the independent laborer is a bounty on indolence and vice."*

If the pendulum swung too far in the direction of severity and niggardliness in the middle nineteenth century, it may be swinging too far in the direction of laxity and prodigality today. A sweeping subsidization of idleness, such as is proposed by the guaranteed income, would only weaken or destroy all incentive to effort, not only on the part of those who were subsidized and supported, but on the part of those who would be forced to support them out of their own earnings. There could be no faster way to impoverish the nation.

Clearly the great problem today is how to keep relief from getting out of hand. But how can we withhold relief from those who would merely rest idly back on it as a permanent way of life, and yet extend it to those who would use it to get back on their feet and once more become productive citizens? This is the baffling problem that I cannot hope to deal with here in detail. Our cities may find themselves compelled to return to some of the safeguards of former days that they perhaps too lightly abandoned—careful tests of needs and means and resources; aid in kind rather than in cash to make sure that the relief meets the particular needs it

*See "Poor Law," *Encyclopedia Britannica*, 1965.

was intended to meet, particularly of children; a restoration of a residential requirement, to prevent people
from moving to a city just to get immediately on its
relief roll and to get more than in some other city; an
obligation to do some sort of useful work in return for
relief until a suitable private job can be found.

But there is a further way to hold down the relief
rolls, and outstanding liberals of former days did not
hesitate to recommend it. In 1914, A. V. Dicey, the eminent British jurist, asked whether it is wise to allow
recipients of poor relief to retain the right to join in the
election of a member of Parliament. And John Stuart
Mill, writing in his *Representative Government* in 1861,
did not equivocate:

I regard it as required by first principles that the receipt
of parish relief should be a preemptory disqualification for
the franchise. He who cannot by his labor suffice for his own
support has no claim to the privilege of helping himself to the
money of others. By becoming dependent on the remaining
members of the community for actual subsistence, he abdi-
cates his claim to equal rights with them in other respects.

In fact, Mill went much further, and insisted that no
one should have the right to vote unless he paid direct
taxes:

It is also important that the assembly which votes the taxes,
either general or local, should be elected exclusively by those
who pay something towards the taxes imposed. Those who
pay no taxes, disposing by their votes of other people's
money, have every motive to be lavish and none to econo-
mize. . . . It amounts to allowing them to put their hands into
other people's pockets for any purpose which they think fit
to call a public one.

In the political climate of today, anyone proposing that the right of franchise be suspended even for those on relief and merely for the time they remained on relief would be derided as having lost touch with political realities. Yet as long as the great and growing army now on various forms of relief and welfare programs retain the right to vote for those who promise them still more of other people's money, we may expect to see relief and welfare programs grow to the point where they eventually undermine the currency and bring on national bankruptcy. The reader will not find it difficult to think of countries where this has already happened.

The Cure Is Production

One of the worst features of all the plans for sharing the wealth and equalizing or guaranteeing incomes is that they lose sight of the conditions and institutions that are necessary to create wealth and income in the first place. They take for granted the existing size of the economic pie; and in their impatient effort to see that it is sliced more equally they overlook the forces that have not only created the pie in the first place but have been baking a larger one year by year. Economic progress and justice do not consist in superbly equalized destitution, but in the constant creation of more and more goods and services, of more and more wealth and income to be shared.

The only real cure for poverty is production.

The way to maximize production is to maximize the incentives to production. And the way to do that, as the modern world has discovered, is through the system known as capitalism—the system of private property, free markets, and free enterprise. This system maximizes production because it allows a man freedom in the choice of his occupation, freedom in his choice of those with whom he associates and cooperates, and, above all, freedom to earn and to keep the fruits of his labor. In the capitalist system each of us, with whatever exceptions, tends in the long run to get what he creates or helps to create. When each of us recognizes that his reward depends on his own efforts and output, and tends to be proportionate to his output, then each has the maximum incentive to increase his effort and output.

Fight Poverty With Capitalism

Capitalism brought the Industrial Revolution, and the enormous increase in productivity that this has made possible. Capitalism has enormously raised the economic level of the masses. It has wiped out whole areas of poverty, and continues to wipe out more. The so-called "pockets of poverty" constantly get smaller and fewer.

The condition of poverty, moreover, is relative rather than absolute. What we call poverty in the United States would be regarded as affluence in most parts of Africa, Asia, or Latin America. If an income sufficient to enable a man "to live with dignity" ought to be "guaranteed" as a matter of "absolute right," why don't the advocates of a guaranteed income insist that this right be enforced first of all in the poor countries, such as India and China, where the need is most widespread and glaring? The reason is simply that even the better-off groups in these nations have not produced enough wealth and income to be expropriated and distributed to others.

One of the guaranteed–income advocates, in a footnote, admits naively: "We must also recognize that we still have no strategy for the elimination of poverty in the underdeveloped countries." Of course they haven't. The "strategy" would be the introduction of free enterprise, and of incentives to work, to save, to accumulate capital, better tools and equipment, and to produce.

But would-be income guarantors ignore or despise the capitalistic system that makes their dreams dreamable and gives their redistribute-the-income proposals whatever plausibility they have. The capitalist system has made this country the most productive and richest in the world. It has continued to achieve its miracles even in the present generation, and to increase them year by year. It has raised the average weekly factory wage from less than $17 in 1933 to $130 in 1969. Even after the rise in prices is allowed for, it has nearly tripled our real per capita disposable income—from $893 in 1933 to $2,473 in 1968 (in 1958 prices).

Allowed to continue to operate with even the relative freedom that it has enjoyed in recent years, the capitalist system will continue to produce these miracles. It will continue to make progress against poverty by a *general* increase in income and wealth. But shortsighted and impatient efforts to wipe out poverty by severing the connection between effort and reward can only lead to the growth of a totalitarian state, and destroy the economic progress that this country has so dearly bought.

Postscript

In his television talk of August 8, 1969, President Nixon announced a giant step deeper into the quagmire of the Welfare State.

What he proposed was the form of the guaranteed annual income known as the negative income tax, plus a couple of additional gimmicks.

He put forward this radical proposal in the language

of conservatism. He said that the last third of a century had "produced a bureaucratic monstrosity" and "left us a legacy of entrenched programs." Then he proposed a plan that can only make the bureaucratic monstrosity more monstrous and create still bigger and more entrenched programs.

He talked about a welfare quagmire with increasing caseloads and escalating costs. He expressed his alarm that "in the past eight years, three million more people have been added to the welfare rolls." And then he proposed a program that would cost no less than $4 billion in the first year alone, and would more than double the number of people eligible for public assistance—from a little under 10 million to more than 22 million.

What additional taxes would be necessary to pay this extra $4 billion was not stated. The President contented himself with the casual remark that the costs would not begin until the fiscal year 1971, "when I expect the funds to be available within the budget." So nobody need worry, even though Congress is now proposing tax *reductions* for that and later years.

Notwithstanding the tremendous differences in prevailing incomes, wage levels and living-cost levels between city and country districts, or between New York and Mississippi, a family of four with no outside income, no matter what state it lives in, would receive under the new plan a minimum Federal payment of $1,600 a year. The states could supplement that amount. The same family could earn as much as $60 a month, or $720 a year, with no loss of benefits. Beyond that, aid would be reduced 50 cents for each dollar earned until the family's income reached $3,920.

There would be no "demeaning investigations." Applicants would simply make declarations of need and begin receiving payments.

The great safeguard, which is supposed to keep the

nation from going into bankruptcy, is that the plan is to
encourage—even force—people to work. Every recipient deemed employable would have to accept a job
deemed suitable by the government or would have to
undergo training.

The long-term outlook for this program is about as
follows:

It is likely to be enacted more or less in the form
President Nixon has proposed, though perhaps a little
bigger. The Republicans in Congress will vote for it as
a matter of party regularity. The chief efforts of the
Democrats, who represent the party of ever-bigger
welfare handouts, will be devoted to trying to increase
the benefits and decrease the safeguards.

No sooner will the program have been enacted than
efforts will be made to enlarge it. We need merely look
at the history of unemployment insurance and of Social
Security, both of which were launched in the Thirties.
Both were originally enacted on the same argument as
the new guaranteed-income proposal: they would make
direct relief unnecessary and so displace it. But not only
has direct relief multiplied steadily, despite growing
prosperity, but unemployment insurance benefits have
constantly grown bigger and longer, and Social Security
benefits have been increased every one or two years
(especially election years) and the coverage constantly
widened.

So every year or two guaranteed income will grow.
First of all, it will be argued that a family of four cannot
be expected to live in decency and dignity on a mere
$1,600 a year. This is less than half of the present quasi-
official poverty-line income. So the basic subsidy will
gradually be pushed up to $3,200 or $3,500 a year,
which means that the top combination of earned income and government benefit will move from $3,920 a
year to $7,720 or more.

Next, few people on relief will be declared to be

employable. Those who are will find very few jobs that
they deem "suitable." They may consent to take gov-
ernment-financed "training" programs, particularly if
they are paid $30 a month for consenting, but many of
them will merely go through the motions. In any case,
the government-administered programs will fall far
short of the kind of training in necessary skills provided
by the old-fashioned apprentice system in private industry. Most certain of all, the whole program of trying
to force people to work for their benefit payments will
be denounced as a sort of slavery. The work requirement will soon be quietly shelved.

The burden of taxation will steadily be increased to
pay for the rising benefits. The attempt will be made to
place the increased burden mainly on corporations and
the high individual incomes. This will further erode
incentives and discourage the production upon which
the welfare of all of us depends. Government expenditures will continue to increase faster than the new tax
revenues, bringing a return to chronic deficits, monetary inflation, and a further fall in the purchasing power
of people's insurance policies, pensions and savings
deposits.

It was not altogether auspicious that President Nixon's announcement of his new guaranteed-income
proposal was made on the evening of the same day that
France was forced to announce another devaluation of
the franc. Like policies, like results.

.\/\.\/\.\/\.\/\.\

CHAPTER 13

Can We Guarantee Jobs?

.\/\.\/\.\/\.\/\.\/\.\/\.\/\.\/\.\/\.\/\.\/\.\/\.\/\.\/\.\/\.\/\.\/\.\/\.\

WHEN A GALLUP POLL IN JUNE, 1968, ASKED PEOPLE whether they favored a guaranteed income for everybody, whether they were willing to work or not, only 36 per cent said yes and 58 per cent were opposed. When the pollsters asked the same people whether the government ought to "guarantee enough work so that each family that has an employable wage earner would be guaranteed enough work each week to give him a wage of about $60 a week or $3,200 a year," 78 per cent answered yes. Only 18 per cent were opposed.

Yet the plausible notion that the government should become the "employer of last resort" would prove as unsound in practice as the guaranteed income without any work attached.

The politicians in power could certainly not afford to be accused of offering even harder jobs or worse conditions than the poorest private employers. Therefore they would have to supply easier jobs and much better conditions, and would probably attract many workers out of existing private marginal jobs into the government-made jobs. For most of those whom the plan would affect, the government would in fact become the employer of first resort.

There is already a demand for workers for the jobs that need to be done, and for which employers are willing and able to pay the legal minimum wage. The government would therefore either have to invent jobs that do not need to be done, or at least are not worth having done at the minimum wage.

The invented jobs, moreover, would have to be where the jobless were. The government could not announce that there were plenty of guaranteed jobs in the forests of Alaska for the slum dwellers of New York City —unless it also provided guaranteed transportation for the workers, their families and their furniture, and guaranteed their housing, supermarkets, schools and other living conditions.

Under such a program it is obvious that most of the made work would be pointless and useless, and most of the made jobs needless and phony.

That is not the end. Suppose the workers with guaranteed jobs were incapable of learning to perform them, or created far more spoilage than useable production? Suppose they habitually showed up an hour or two late, or took three hours for lunch, or came in only to collect their pay, or ignored all instructions, or were unruly, or committed acts of sabotage and vandalism, or kicked the boss downstairs? Their jobs would be guaranteed, wouldn't they?

Anyone who thinks I am imagining problems need

merely read the details of the riot of 1,500 youngsters outside New York's City Hall on July 10, 1968. They were protesting cutbacks in the city's projected summer job program. I quote the account in the New York *Times:*

Some of the youngsters (most of them teen-agers from the city's white, Negro and Puerto Rican poverty areas) smashed six automobiles parked outside City Hall, hurled rocks, bottles and broken glass at the police and looted frankfurter wagons and newsstands in the area. At the height of the disturbance, bands of youngsters fanned out from City Hall Park, smashed several windows in the nearby Woolworth Building and knocked down and robbed a 50-year-old woman.

These tactics were rewarded handsomely. The very next day Mayor John Lindsay announced that the city would appropriate $5 million for more summer jobs. Before that he had repeatedly asserted that no city money was available for such jobs.

All this doesn't mean that the problem of providing more real jobs for the unskilled and for teen-agers is insoluble. As some eminent economists have already pointed out, the most important step would be to repeal the existing Federal minimum wage law.

CHAPTER 14

Soaking the Rich

EVERYWHERE WE TURN TODAY WE FIND THE WEL-fare state—the state that promises guaranteed jobs, guaranteed incomes, the guaranteed life, security from cradle to grave, the quick if not overnight elimination of poverty. And the principal way in which it under-takes to achieve these goals is to seize from those who have and give to those who have not.

The main instrument it uses for this purpose is the graduated income tax. In the United States this tax has been imposed since 1913. In the beginning it seemed innocent enough. The top rate was only 7 per cent. But in 1925 the top rate had gone to 25 per cent; in 1935 to 63 per cent; in 1940 to 81 per cent; in 1945 to 94 per cent. In the tax cut of 1964 the top rate was reduced to 70 per cent. With the 1968 surcharge it went up again to 77 per cent.

In today's world these confiscatory rates are not exceptional. The First National City Bank of New York recently compiled a table comparing the highest marginal income tax rates in fifteen countries. The rates (after rounding out fractions) are: Italy 95 per cent, United Kingdom 91, Canada 82, United States 77, France 76, Japan 75, Netherlands 71, Austria 69, Australia 68, Belgium 66, Sweden 65, West Germany 55, Denmark 53, Norway 50, and Switzerland 8.

It would be misleading to assume that these top-rate figures necessarily reflect the overall comparative tax levels in these countries. Italy's 95 per cent rate applies only to incomes above $800,000, whereas Norway's 50 per cent rate applies to all incomes above $13,000. Though Sweden's top income tax rate is in the lower half of the list, Sweden imposes the heaviest comparative tax load in the world.

What the comparisons do show graphically is how almost universal the soak-the-rich tax philosophy has now become. An elaborate rationalization, on grounds of "social justice" and "ability to pay," has been built up for progressive tax rates since the beginning of this century; but economists are at last beginning to recognize that all arguments in support of progression can be used to justify any degree of progression.

Certainly there is no evidence that the steeply progressive rates have helped the poor. On the contrary, these confiscatory rates clearly undermine incentives, reduce production and capital accumulation, and leave less to be shared by everybody.

The earliest sponsors of the progressive income tax recognized this, but they had other aims in mind. In the Communist Manifesto of 1848, Marx and Engels frankly proposed "a heavy progressive or graduated income tax" as an instrument by which "the proletariat will use its political supremacy to wrest, by degrees, all capital from the bourgeois, to centralize all instruments of production in the hands of the State," and to make "despotic inroads on the right of property, and on the conditions of bourgeois production."

Progressive rates of income taxation are not necessary to raise great revenues. A simple calculation, based on the Treasury's own figures for 1966, shows that, with the same existing exemptions and deductions, a flat rate of 19.6 per cent would have raised all the revenue raised from the scale of rates ranging from 14 to 70 per cent.

On a similar calculation, if all the rates now above 50 per cent were reduced to that level, then (on the basis of 1965 income tax returns) a maximum of $373 million would be lost. This is not enough to run the government, at present spending rates, for a single day. If all incomes over $100,000 were taxed at a rate of 100 per cent, the maximum revenue *gain* would be $200 million.

For 1965, 70 per cent of the total income tax was paid by people with adjusted gross incomes under $20,000, for the simple reason that these people constituted 97.5 per cent of all income tax payers, and that they collectively reported more than 80 per cent of the country's taxable income.

It is not only in the United States that the actual revenue yield from the higher income tax rates is negligible. In Great Britain, in the fiscal year 1964-65, total government revenues were £8,157 million, the revenue from the personal income tax £3,088 million, and the revenue from the surtax £184 million. In other words, the revenue from all the surtax rates (ranging above the standard rate of 41¼ per cent up to 96¼ per cent) yielded less than 6 per cent of all revenue from the income tax, and barely more than 2 per cent of Britain's total revenues.

In Sweden, in 1963, individuals paid first a local proportional income tax averaging about 15 per cent; then on the rest of their income, they paid progressive national taxes ranging from 10 to 65 per cent. A study published by the Swedish Taxpayers' Association found that the basic national income tax rate of 10 per cent brought in about 70 per cent of the total national income tax revenue; that if the maximum national rate had stopped at 25 per cent, the tax would have brought in 90 per cent of its then revenue; and that if the maximum rate had stopped at 45 per cent, the government would have received 99 per cent of its actual revenue. In short, the study found that the rates between 45 and 65 per cent brought in only 1 per cent of the total national income tax revenue.

The unavoidable conclusion is that the progressive rates of income tax everywhere, and especially those above 50 per cent, are imposed not to raise revenue, but merely to satisfy vindictiveness and envy.

Yet perhaps the most serious evil of the progressive income tax is that it produces the *illusion* in the overwhelming majority of taxpayers that the "rich"—meaning the people in the brackets above them—are really paying for most of the benefits that the majority gets from the government. This illusion is probably shared in the United States even by single taxpayers with taxable income just above $7,000, who are in fact paying more than the 21 per cent average rate that yielded the fiscal 1969 revenue. This illusion leads them to accept complacently a burden of government expenditure and taxation that they would not otherwise tolerate.

Though this aspect of progressive income taxation

receives practically no attention today, its menace was
recognized as early as 1899 by W. E. H. Lecky:

Highly graduated taxation realizes most completely the
supreme danger of democracy, creating a state of things in
which one class imposes on another burdens which it is not
asked to share, and impels the State into vast schemes of
extravagance, under the belief that the whole costs will be
thrown upon others.

CHAPTER 15

Soaking the Corporations

PERSONAL INCOME TAX RATES THAT RISE TO THE level of 77 per cent obviously discourage incentives, investment, and production. But no politician raises the point for fear that he will be accused of defending the rich. What is probably an even greater discouragement to new investment and increased production is the present marginal corporation income tax of 52.8 per cent. Yet this gets even less criticism than high personal income taxes. Nobody wants to defend the corporations. They are everybody's whipping boy. And yet they are the key productive element on which the nation's income, wealth and economic growth depend.

There was at least some awareness of this until recent years. When the tax on corporation income was first imposed, in 1913, it was at the very cautious rate of 1 per cent. This was also raised very cautiously. Even in World War I the rate was lifted only to 12 per cent. It never got above 15 per cent until 1937. In the midst of World War II it was still only 40 per cent. It did not get to 52 per cent until 1952.

Today such a rate is taken for granted. Yet the people who approve of it, and who suggest maybe it could be a little higher, are the very people who have been complaining most loudly in recent years about the country's disappointing rate of economic growth.

The steep rate of tax on corporate income gets so little criticism because there is confusion of thought concerning whom it falls on and what are its economic effects. Is the whole tax "absorbed" by the corporation, for instance, or is part or all of it "shifted"?

What happens is somewhat complicated. A corporation is a legal fiction. From an investment standpoint, it consists of its present stockholders. When the tax on corporations is raised above its preceding level, most of the loss falls on existing stockholders in the form of a capital loss—and later of an income loss. If, to simplify, we can imagine a situation in which a corporation were wholly free from taxation, and then suddenly a 50 per cent income tax (assumed to be permanent) were imposed on its future earnings, the price of its shares would tend to fall in the stock market by 50 per cent. The old shareholders would be forced to absorb the loss in capital value and in future income. The new buyers, however, able to buy the stock for half of its former market price, would stand to get the prevailing "normal" return on their capital investment.

Even for the new buyers, however, this would apply only to their original investment. When the corporation management considered any *new* investment, any corporate expansion, any addition to plant or equipment, it would have to consider the tax. And this would apply, of course, to anybody who thought of launching an entirely new corporation.

The present average tax on all corporations is about 45 per cent. On successful corporations of any size, however, the average rate is close to 52 per cent. Broadly speaking, therefore, when anybody contemplates a *new* corporate investment, he will not make it unless the investment promises to yield *before taxes* at least *twice* as much as the net return he would consider worthwhile. If, for example, he would not consider a new investment worthwhile unless it promised a 10 per cent average annual return on his capital outlay, then it would have to promise a return of 20 per cent on that outlay before taxes.

It is obvious that a corporation income tax in the neighborhood of 50 per cent must drastically reduce the incentive to new investment, and therefore to the consequent increase in jobs, real wages, and economic growth that the politicians are always calling for.

But what is at least as important as reducing the incentive to investment, the present corporate tax reduces the funds available for investment. In 1968, according to estimates of the Department of Commerce, United States corporations earned total profits before taxes of $91.1 billion. Out of this their corporate tax liability was $41.3 billion. This reduced their profits after taxes to $49.8 billion. Out of this sum, in turn, $23.1 billion was paid out in dividends while $26.7 billion was retained in undistributed profits.

This last figure represents the corporations' own reinvestment of their earnings in working capital, inventories, improvements, new plants and equipment. If there had been no corporate tax, and there had been the same proportionate distribution of profits between dividends and reinvestment, the amount of money reinvested would have been $50.5 billion instead of $26.7 billion—89 per cent, or $23.8 billion, greater. A proportional increase in dividends would have given stockholders about $20 billion more than they actually received. If they reinvest only a fifth of what they receive in dividends, this would make an annual increase in corporate investment in the neighborhood of $25 billion.

Of course certain deductions would have to be made from this figure if we tried to calculate what would be lost from investment by alternate taxes imposed to raise the same revenue. But broadly speaking, the overwhelming bulk of annual government expenditure goes into current consumption rather than in building up the capital formation, the economic strength and wealth-and-income-producing capacity of the country.

A great deal of the complacency about our drastic corporation tax stems from the idea that the tax is somehow "shifted" to others. One common facile assumption is that the corporations just pass the tax along by raising their prices. How they can do this so easily is never explained.

Nor is it prima facie plausible. Every television manufacturer, for instance, must keep his prices competitive with other television manufacturers. Granted, they all pay about the same percentage tax on their net profits. Yet all of them must also keep their prices competitive with those of foreign manufacturers. The same is true of automobile companies and, in fact, of all American companies that either have an export market or must meet competition from imports.

A uniform sales or excise tax (if also imposed on imports) can be passed along uniformly, but not a percentage tax on profits after expenses, because this necessarily means *a different tax rate per unit of output* on every producer. Its general tendency is to penalize the low-cost efficient producer much more than the high-cost inefficient producer.

There is one reason, however, why over a long period a higher corporate income tax can be passed along in a price rise. This is because the tax may eventually put some manufacturers out of business, prevent others from expanding, and certainly retard the expansion of the rest. It will force those who stay in business to keep decrepit and obsolete machinery much longer than otherwise. It will retard or prevent reduction in costs. It will reduce supply, raise production costs, and make quality and variety poorer than they otherwise would be. The consumers of the country will be more poorly served.

The end result in this case, however, is not so much that the corporate income tax is "shifted" as that an *additional* burden is placed on the whole country. By discouraging and retarding investment in new machinery and plants, either by existing corporations or by the formation of new corporations, the 52.8 per cent corporation income tax shields existing obsolescent capacity from the competition of the new, more modern and efficient plant and equipment that would otherwise come into existence, or that would come into existence much sooner.

By striking directly at new investment, the present corporate income tax slows down economic growth more directly and surely than does any other tax.

The only study I can at present think of that has adequately explained the devastating effect of the high corporate income tax on investment appeared in a pamphlet by Dr. George Terborgh for the Machinery and Allied Products Institute of Washington in 1959. It left no traceable influence on Congress or the Treasury.

The tax, by hurting business and investment, hurts employment and slows down the increase in productivity and in real wages. In brief, in the long run it hurts most of all the mass of the country's workers.

/\\/\\/\\/\\

CHAPTER 16

Government Planning vs. Economic Growth

/\\

WHEN WE DISCUSS "ECONOMIC PLANNING," WE MUST be clear concerning what it is we are talking about. The real question being raised is not: plan or no plan? but *whose* plan?

Each of us, in his private capacity, is constantly planning for the future: what he will do the rest of today, the rest of the week, or on the weekend; what he will do this month or next year. Some of us are planning, though in a more general way, ten or twenty years ahead.

We are making these plans in our capacity both as consumers and as producers. Employees are either planning to stay where they are, or to shift from one job to another, or from one company to another, or from one city to another, or even from one career to another. Entrepreneurs are either planning to stay in one location or to move to another, to expand or contract their operations, to stop making a product for which they think demand is dying and to start making one for which they think demand is going to grow.

Now the people who call themselves Economic Planners either ignore or by implication deny all this. They talk as if the world of private enterprise, the free market, supply, demand, and competition, were a world of chaos and anarchy, in which nobody ever planned ahead, but merely drifted or staggered along. I once engaged in a television debate with an eminent Planner in a high official position who implied that without his forecasts and guidance American business would be "flying blind." At best, the Planners imply, the world of private enterprise is one in which everybody works or plans at cross-purposes or makes his plans solely in his "private" interest rather than in the "public" interest.

Now the Planner wants to substitute his own plan for the plans of everybody else. At best, he wants the *government* to lay down a Master Plan to which everybody else's plan must be subordinated.

Planning Means Compulsion

It is this aspect of Planning to which our attention should be directed: Planning always involves *compulsion*. This may be disguised in various ways. The government Planners will, of course, try to persuade people that the Master Plan has been drawn up for their own good, and that the only persons who are going to be coerced are those whose plans are "not in the public interest."

The Planners will say, in the newly fashionable

phraseology, that their plans are not "imperative," but merely "indicative." They will make a great parade of "democracy," freedom, cooperation, and noncompulsion by "consulting all groups"—"Labor," "Industry," the Government, even "Consumers' Representatives" — in drawing up the Master Plan and the specific "goals" or "targets." Of course, if they could really succeed in giving everybody his proportionate weight and voice and freedom of choice, if everybody were allowed to pursue the plan of production or consumption of specific goods and services that he had intended to pursue or would have pursued anyway, then the whole Plan would be useless and pointless, a complete waste of energy and time. The Plan would be meaningful only if it forced the production and consumption of *different* things or different quantities of things than a free market would have provided. In short, it would be meaningful only insofar as it put compulsion on *somebody* and forced some change in the pattern of production and consumption.

There are two excuses for this coercion. One is that the free market produces the *wrong* goods, and that only government Planning and direction can assure the production of the "right" ones. This is the thesis popularized by J. K. Galbraith. The other excuse is that the free market does not produce *enough* goods, and that only government Planning can speed things up. This is the thesis of the apostles of "economic growth."

The Galbraith Thesis

Let us take up the "Galbraith" thesis first. I put his name in quotation marks because the thesis long antedates his presentation of it. It is the basis of all the Communist "Five-Year Plans," which are now aped by a score of socialist nations. While these Plans may consist in setting out some general overall percentage of production increase, their characteristic feature is rather a whole network of specific "targets" for specific industries: there is to be a 25 per cent increase in steel capacity, a 15 per cent increase in cement production, a 12 per cent increase in butter and milk output, and so forth.

There is always a strong bias in these Plans, especially in the Communist countries, in favor of heavy industry, because it gives increased power to make war. In all the Plans, moreover, even in non-Communist countries, there is a strong bias in favor of industrialization, of heavy industry as against agriculture, in the belief that this necessarily increases real income faster and leads to greater national self-sufficiency. It is not an accident that such countries are constantly running into agricultural crises and food famines.

But the Plans also reflect either the implied or explicit moral judgments of the government Planners. The latter seldom plan for an increased production of cigarettes or whiskey or, in fact, of any so-called "luxury" item. The standards are always grim and puritanical. The word "austerity" makes a chronic appearance. Consumers are told that they must "tighten their belts" for a little longer. Sometimes, if the last Plan has not been too unsuccessful, there is a little relaxation: consumers can, perhaps, have a few more motor cars and hospitals and playgrounds. But there is almost never any provision for, say, more golf courses or even bowling alleys. In general, no form of expenditure is approved that cannot be universalized, or at least "majoritized." And such so-called luxury expenditure is discouraged, even in a so-called "indicative" Plan, by not allowing access by promotors of such projects to bank credit or to the capital markets. At some point government coercion or compulsion comes into play.

This disapproval and coercion may rest on several grounds. Nearly all "austerity" programs stem from the belief, not that the person who wants to make a "luxury" expenditure cannot afford it, but that "the nation" cannot afford it. This involves the assumption that, if I set up a bowling alley or patronize one, I am somehow depriving my fellow citizens of more necessary goods or services. This would be true only on the assumption that the proper thing to do is to tax my so-called surplus income away from me and turn it over to others in the form of money, goods, or services. But if I am allowed to keep my "surplus" income, and am forbidden to spend it on bowling alleys or on imported wine and cheese, I will spend it on something else that is not forbidden. Thus when the British austerity program after World War II prevented an Englishman from consuming imported luxuries, on the ground that "the nation" could not afford the "foreign exchange" or the "unfavorable balance of payments," officials were shocked to find that the money was being squandered on football pools or dog races. And there is no reason to suppose, in any case, that the "dollar shortage" or the "unfavorable balance of payments" was helped in the least. The austerity program, insofar as it was not enforced by higher income taxes, probably cut down potential exports as much as it did potential imports; and insofar as it was enforced by higher income taxes, it discouraged exports by restricting and discouraging production.

But we come now to the specific Galbraith thesis, growing out of the age-long bureaucratic suspicion of luxury spending, that consumers generally do not know how to spend the income they have earned; that they buy whatever advertisers tell them to buy; that consumers are, in short, boobs and suckers, chronically wasting

their money on trivialities, if not on absolute trash. The
bulk of consumers also, if left to themselves, show atro-
cious taste, and crave cerise automobiles with ridiculous tailfins.

The natural conclusion from all this—and Galbraith
does not hesitate to draw it—is that consumers ought to
be deprived of freedom of choice, and that government
bureaucrats, full of wisdom—of course, of a very *un-
conventional* wisdom—should make their consumptive
choices for them. The consumers should be supplied,
not with what they themselves want, but with what
bureaucrats of exquisite taste and culture think is good
for them. And the way to do this is to tax away from
people all the income they have been foolish enough to
earn above that required to meet their bare necessities,
and turn it over to the bureaucrats to be spent in ways
which the latter think would really do people the most
good—more and better roads and parks and playgrounds and schools and television programs—all supplied, of course, by government.

"Private" vs. "Public" Sector

And here Galbraith resorts to a neat semantic trick.
The goods and services for which people voluntarily
spend their own money make up, in his vocabulary, the
"private sector" of the economy, while the goods and
services supplied to them by the government, out of the
income it has seized from them in taxes, make up the
"public sector." Now the adjective "private" carries an
aura of the selfish and exclusive, the inward-looking,
whereas the adjective "public" carries an aura of the
democratic, the shared, the generous, the patriotic, the
outward-looking—in brief, the public-spirited. And as
the tendency of the expanding welfare state has been,

in fact, to take out of private hands and more and more take into its own hands provision of the goods and services that are considered to be most essential and most edifying—roads and water supply, schools and hospitals and scientific research, education, old-age insurance and medical care—the tendency must be increasingly to associate the word "public" with everything that is really necessary and laudable, leaving the "private sector" to be associated merely with the superfluities and capricious wants and vices that are left over after everything that is really important has been taken care of.

If the distinction between the two "sectors" were put in more neutral terms—say, the "private sector" versus the "governmental sector"—the scales would not be so heavily weighted in favor of the latter. In fact, this more neutral vocabulary would raise in the mind of the hearer the question whether certain activities now assumed by the modern welfare state do legitimately or appropriately come within the governmental province. For Galbraith's use of the word "sector," "private" or "public," cleverly carries the implication that the public "sector" is legitimately not only whatever the government has already taken over but a great deal besides. Galbraith's whole point is that the "public sector" is "starved" in favor of a "private sector" overstuffed with superfluities and trash.

The true distinction, and the appropriate vocabulary, however, would throw an entirely different light on the matter. What Galbraith calls the "private sector" of the economy is, in fact, the *voluntary* sector; and what he calls the "public sector" is, in fact, the *coercive* sector. The voluntary sector is made up of the goods and services for which people voluntarily spend the money they have earned. The coercive sector is made up of the goods and services that are provided, regardless of the

wishes of the individual, out of the taxes that are seized
from him. And as this sector grows at the expense of the
voluntary sector, we come to the essence of the welfare
state. In this state nobody pays for the education of his
own children but everybody pays for the education of
everybody else's children. Nobody pays his own medical bills, but everybody pays everybody else's medical
bills. Nobody helps his elderly parents, but everybody
else's elderly parents. Nobody provides for the contin-
gency of his own unemployment, his own sickness, his
own old age, but everybody provides for the unemployment, sickness, or old age of everybody else. The welfare state, as Bastiat put it with uncanny clairvoyance
more than a century ago, is the great fiction by which
everybody tries to live at the expense of everybody
else.

This is not only a fiction; it is bound to be a failure.
This is sure to be the outcome whenever effort is sepa-
rated from reward. When people who earn more than
the average have their "surplus," or the greater part of
it, seized from them in taxes, and when people who
earn less than the average have the deficiency, or the
greater part of it, turned over to them in handouts and
doles, the production of all must sharply decline; for the
energetic and able lose their incentive to produce more
than the average, and the slothful and unskilled lose
their incentive to improve their condition.

The Growth Planners

I have spent so much space in analyzing the fallacies
of the Galbraithian school of Economic Planners that I
have left myself little in which to analyze the fallacies
of the Growth Planners. Many of their fallacies are the
same; but there are some important differences.

The chief difference is that the Galbraithians believe that a free market economy produces too much (though, of course, they are the "wrong" goods), whereas the Growthmen believe that a free market economy does not produce nearly enough. I will postpone for the moment discussion of some of the *statistical* errors, gaps, and fallacies in their arguments. Here I want to concentrate on their idea that some form of government direction or coercion can by some strange magic increase production above the level that can be achieved when everybody enjoys economic freedom.

It seems to me self-evident that when people are free, production tends to be, if not maximized, at least optimized. This is because, in a system of free markets and private property, everybody's reward tends to equal the value of his production. What he gets for his production (and is allowed to keep) is in fact what it is worth in the market. If he wants to double his income in a single year, he is free to try—and may succeed if he is able to double his contribution to production in a single year. If he is content with the income he has— if he feels that he can only get more by excessive effort or risk—he is under no pressure to increase his output. In a free market everyone is free to maximize his satisfactions, whether these consist in more leisure or in more goods.

But along comes the Growth Planner. He finds by statistics (whose trustworthiness and accuracy he never doubts) that the economy has been growing, say, only 2.8 per cent a year. He concludes, in a flash of genius, that a growth rate of 5 per cent a year would be faster. How does he propose to achieve this?

There is among the Growth Planners a profound mystical belief in the power of words. They declare that they "are not satisfied" with a growth rate of a mere 2.8 per cent a year. And once having spoken, they act as if half the job had already been done. If they did not assume this, it would be impossible to explain the deep earnestness with which they argue among themselves whether the growth rate "ought" to be 4 or 5 or 6 per cent. (The only thing they always agree on is that it ought to be greater than whatever it actually is.) Having decided on this magic overall figure, they then proceed either to set specific targets for specific goods (and here they are at one with the Russian Five-Year Planners) or to announce some general recipe for reaching the overall rate.

But why do they assume that setting their magic target rate will increase the rate of production over the existing one? And how is their growth rate supposed to apply as far as the individual is concerned? Is the man who is already making $50,000 a year to be coerced into working for an income of $52,500 next year? Is the man who is making only $5,000 a year to be forbidden to make more than $5,250 next year? If not, what is gained by making a specific "annual growth rate" a governmental "target"? Why not just permit or encourage everybody to do his best, or make his own decision, and let the average "growth" be whatever it turns out to be?

Statistical Fallacies

Now let us get back to some of the statistical errors and fallacies that I mentioned a little while back.

One of them will be plain from what we have just been discussing. This is the fallacy of speaking of a "national" rate of growth. The ambiguity of this should be evident. A gross rate of growth of national income may appear in the official statistics accompanied by an increase in the population of the country. One can have a growth in gross national product (GNP) accompanied by a *fall* in *per capita* incomes. Even aside from this, it should be obvious that an *average* increase in per capita incomes in a country does not necessarily tell us much regarding the fate of individuals. An average increase in per capita incomes may mask a fall in the incomes of some groups if this is more than offset by a rise in the incomes of others. For example, if the rich got richer and the poor got poorer, the average per capita figures might still conceivably show a rise.

Again, there are several pitfalls in dealing with percentage figures. The smaller the base from which we start, the less the absolute increase in the production of anything has to be in order to show a very large percentage increase. To begin with an extreme example, if only one family in a country has a bathtub, and the next year fifty families get one, the rate of growth is 5,000 per cent. But once everybody in that country has a bathtub, net growth may stop. This principle applies to houses, automobiles, radios, television sets, and everything else. From the day of his birth, a boy baby grows in weight an average of 195 per cent in his first year. He never even approaches this record thereafter.

It should not be surprising that there has been found to be a long-run tendency for industrial growth rates to slow down as the level of production in any country gets higher. This results partly from the enlargement of the base, and partly from a physical satiation point in human needs.

Let us take the history of a specific economic product —television. Output of television sets in the United States in 1946 was 7,000. In 1947 this output had risen to 200,000, making a growth rate of 2,757 per cent. In 1948 the United States produced 975,000 sets—making a growth rate of only 387 per cent. In 1949 output rose to 3,029,000 sets—but the growth rate was only 211 per cent. In 1950 production jumped to 7,464,000 sets; but the growth rate now was only 146 per cent. Though output was accelerating enormously in absolute *amounts, percentage* rates of growth were constantly *falling.* And after 1950 the *rate* of growth of annual output for a time *stopped entirely.* Yet the United States continued to turn out between 6 million and 11 million sets a year—and, of course, now has the highest total number of sets working, old and new, in its history. As of 1967, these were estimated to total 94.2 million. Yet many other countries in the world must now be surpassing the United States' *rate* of growth in this particular product. The more backward the country, probably the higher the present growth rate in production or purchase of television sets.

Not Volume but Value

Suppose we turn now to some of the more basic general problems raised in the compilation of total gross national output figures. The first thing we have to remember is that these are not and cannot be purely objective figures. What we are measuring is not physical volume or weight, but *value.* The statistician is forced to resort to his own arbitrary values. Shall he include, for example, in the national income figures the compensation of burglars, blackmailers, and drug peddlers? How is he to draw the line between what are usually called economic goods and such activities as washing, shaving, and playing for amusement on the piano? Yet such activities do not differ from the same activities carried on for money as services to other people—such as nursing, barbering, and giving concerts. The statistician is forced to include only items that are dealt in on the market.* But this excludes all do-it-yourself activities,

*See Simon Kuznets, *National Income and Its Composition, 1919-1938* (New York: National Bureau of Economic Research, 1941), 2 vols.

which in total are probably enormous, and it excludes all the products of the family economy, including all the activities of housewives. So we get the paradox, for example, that when a man marries his cook, the value of her work disappears from the national income accounts.

But there are further problems. How is the statistician to treat government activities? Official figures practically always do include these in making up the national income accounts. But there is no market test or gauge of their value. Most people would admit that policemen, firemen, and judges make a contribution to the national income equivalent to the cost of their services. But how about a host of bureaucrats whose activities might merely redistribute income, or might actually restrain and disrupt production through imposition or enforcement of unwise regulations?

Again, how do we count government redistribution of income through subsidized housing, farm price supports, Social Security pensions, doles to the unemployed, subsidized medicine, etc.? Most government statisticians count the income that is handed out to the recipients without deducting from the gross national product figures the income that is taxed away from those who are forced to contribute.

To illustrate, let us take an elementary example. Suppose, in a community of three persons, that two persons have an annual income of $3,000 each and the third has no income at all. The community income is $6,000. Now suppose the government levies a tax of a third, or 33 1/3 per cent, on the two persons who have the $3,000 income, and gives the $1,000 that it takes from each of them to the third person. Then these two people have left only an income of $2,000 to match the income of $2,000 given, say, to the unemployed person. The amount of total income in that community is the same as it was before. The disposable income of each person is $2,000; and their total income is $6,000. But many government statisticians would still credit the first two persons with their original earned income of $3,000 each. So that with their earnings of $6,000, plus the $2,000 given to the unemployed person, the three of them would now be credited with a total income of $8,000—an increase of 33 1/3 per cent. Thus redistribution of wealth and social welfare plans almost invariably increase the gross national product *estimate*.

Measuring Leisure and Liberty

But now we come to still another problem in the statistical measurement and comparison of national income or gross national product figures. All these figures measure national *output* multiplied by the monetary value of that output. But they do not measure leisure or the satisfactions of leisure. Yet these are primary concerns in individual welfare. In the United States there is, on the average, a forty-hour working week. A couple of generations ago, there was a sixty- or seventy-hour typical working week. Now a community that can turn out its national product in an average week of forty hours is obviously immensely better off in economic satisfactions than another community of equal numbers that turns out the same physical product but requires a seventy-hour average working week to do it. I will not elaborate upon this, but simply point out that it is only one of the considerations that make any precise comparison of national incomes of different countries invalid.

Of course all economic planning, as we have already seen, must necessarily involve compulsion and coercion —in other words, a loss of liberty on the part of the citizens. This loss of liberty is a substantial cost, which some of us would rank very high; but it is never counted by the economic planners. Again, like the loss of leisure, the loss of liberty is another factor that makes statistical comparisons between, say, the GNP of the United States and Soviet Russia misleading and invalid.

All economic planning by a government involves problems of arbitrary allocation, arbitrary quotas for thousands of commodities and services, allocations of work, and allocations of income and consumption. And among the most serious of these, though the Growth Planners almost never mention it, are what we may call *intertemporal* problems and allocations.* When the Growth Planners decide that we must grow economically 5 or 6 per cent a year, or whatever rate, they are arbitrarily deciding that we are entitled to consume only a certain percentage of our income in any year, and must save and invest the rest in order to have greater production in the future. But is it always and under all conditions desirable to sacrifice the present to the future? Is it always desirable for the present generation to consume less so that people still unborn (whom we do not even know) should consume more? I shall not try to answer this question. I wish merely to point out here that economic growth has a cost—that the higher we wish to make this rate of economic growth, the more we must restrain and constrict consumption in the present to make it possible. This cost is entirely ignored by most of the Growth Planners.

Finally, we have to ask, what is it that is measured by the gross national product figures? What is being measured is the *marginal* market value of thousands of goods and services, in terms of money, multiplied by

*On these intertemporal problems, as well as comparisons of leisure and liberty, see Israel Kirzner, "On the Premises of Growth Economics," *New Individualist Review*, Vol. 3, No. 1 (University of Chicago).

the total quantities of such goods and services. (Of course any inflation of the currency will multiply this figure correspondingly without adding an iota to the economic satisfaction that anybody gets. I will come back to this in a moment.) What I wish to point out here is that if we increase the supply of anything (with the money supply remaining constant), the *marginal* value of that commodity, and hence its price, *falls.* So if there is no inflation of the currency, an increase in production leads to a fall in prices. And this fall in prices is likely to be much greater proportionately than the increase in production. It has been recognized for many years, for example, that a larger wheat crop will ordinarily have a smaller total dollar market value than a smaller crop. This, in fact, is a basis of all crop restriction schemes. But this merely illustrates a wider principle. It is not "value-in-use," but scarcity, that determines "value-in-exchange," or money price. Water is an indispensable commodity that ordinarily commands no price at all. If more and more things became plentiful (except dollars), the national income, as measured in dollars, might begin to *fall.* And if we could imagine a situation in which everything we could wish for were in as adequate supply as air and water, we might have no (monetary) national income at all!

Inflation vs. Growth

Most of the advocates of economic growth through government action in fact put their major faith in one overall policy—inflation.

This policy, however, is almost never recommended under that name. The Growth Planners simply argue (along Keynesian lines) that growth has been slow or business stagnant because of an "insufficiency of aggregate demand"; and they think this can be rectified by more government spending. Some of these Planners are candid enough openly to advocate government deficits. For they recognize that if the increased government spending is paid for out of increased taxation, then the taxpayers lose exactly as much "purchasing power" as the government gains. They also recognize that if the increased government spending is financed by a bond issue bought by individuals out of real savings, the bondbuyers lose as much purchasing power for other things as the government gains.

They recognize, finally, that if the government raises, say, $10 billion in the investment market, this either leaves just that much less funds available for investment in private industry or pushes up interest rates. And high interest rates, other things being equal, discourage business expansion and investment.

So the only way to get the "increased purchasing power" is to increase the money supply. If a country is already frankly on a paper-money basis, it merely runs the printing presses a little faster. If, like the United States, it is on the semblance of a gold standard, it does this through the central bank. The usual process is for the bank to buy government securities in the open market and "monetize" them.

But does the increase in money supply necessarily promote economic growth? If there is *already* full employment and no substantial idle capacity, the new money will simply lead to an increase in wages and prices. If there is less than full employment, the new money can, it is true, at least temporarily increase employment if it leads to an increased demand for products or to higher prices for products *without* also leading to correspondingly increased wage rates.

Those who propose the inflationary solution for unemployment always forget to ask themselves what has caused the unemployment. The long-run cause will always be found to be some discoordination of prices and wages. This can take many forms. Commonly wage rates in some lines will be too high in relation to prices or to the demand for particular products. But wage-price coordination, in such cases, can be restored and maintained if there are free-market wages and free-market prices flexible in both directions. Inflation is not necessary to restore such coordination. Moreover, any price-wage adjustment brought about by inflation is likely to be only temporary. For labor unions, finding more demand for their services, or trying to "catch up" with rising living costs, demand still higher wages, with the result that the discoordination of wages and prices may be brought about all over again, and the situation can be cured once more only by a still further dose of inflation.

As long as the government authorities encourage or tolerate a system that makes it possible for unions constantly to demand and secure uneconomic wage rates, to which prices can be adjusted only by successive doses of inflation, the authorities must encourage the continuance and perpetuation of such discoordination. This must retard economic growth.

Inflation Falsifies Calculation

Inflation is not only unnecessary for economic growth. As long as it exists it is the enemy of economic growth. It distorts and falsifies economic calculation. An economy grows and functions at its maximum rate when the relationship of prices and wages and profits, and the whole balance of production among thousands of different commodities and services are such as to lead toward an equalization of profit margins because of correct anticipations of the relationship of supply and demand, of prices, production and costs.

But when inflation forces up prices, prices do not all rise in the same proportion and at the same rate. It becomes very difficult for business men to distinguish between what is lasting and what is merely temporary, or to know what the real demands of the consumers will be or what the real costs of their own operations are. Orthodox accounting practices will give misleading results. Depreciation and replacement allowances will be inadequate. Profits will be overestimated and overstated. Businessmen everywhere will be deceived. They will be using up their real capital when they think they are increasing it. They will think they have profits or capital gains when they really have losses.

A vital function of the free market is to penalize inefficiency and misjudgment and to reward efficiency and good judgment. By distorting economic calculations and creating illusory profits, inflation will destroy this function. Because nearly everybody will seem to prosper, there will be all sorts of maladjustments and investments in the wrong lines. Honest work and sound production will tend to give way to speculation and gambling. There will be a deterioration in the quality of goods and services and in the real standard of living.

The price and wage rises brought about by inflation will lead to public demands for price and wage controls. The government will be only too receptive to such demands because price and wage controls tacitly put the blame for the inflation on those who are getting the prices and wages rather than on the government's policies. But these price and wage controls will reduce, distort, and disrupt production, and do far more harm than even the inflation itself.

What is likely even before price control is the institution of some sort of exchange control, to prevent the quotation of the home currency from falling in terms of other currencies. But the effect of such an exchange control, overvaluing the domestic currency, will be to bring about a deficit in the balance of payments. It will discourage exports, because they will be overpriced compared with foreign goods. It will encourage imports. The exchange authorities, to prevent this, will institute a quota and licensing system. But this will disrupt foreign trade.

I have yet to mention what many will consider the most important reason of all why inflation must in the long run retard rather than accelerate economic growth. Its effect must be to discourage monetary savings, and to encourage personal spending on immediate consumption. To this extent it must discourage and reduce capital formation, the principal cause of economic growth.

Of course inflation does temporarily stimulate investment in certain directions. When it is going on it makes nearly every venture look profitable in monetary terms. It therefore provides a strong incitement to reinvestment of profits and to the purchase of equity shares (though not of mortgages and bonds). But, as we have already seen, inflation falsifies all the signals and confuses and distorts economic calculation. What it tends to stimulate is *mal*investment. By directing investment into the wrong channels it leads to great waste and must retard properly balanced growth over the long run.

The long-run effect of inflation, in sum, can only be to reduce and distort production and to retard economic growth. Of course this effect can be concealed from many people, perhaps a majority, for a long time. For prices, wages, and incomes will all be constantly going higher in monetary terms. The official gross national product figures will be constantly soaring. The euphoria can temporarily lull all misgivings. But eventually the bitter moment of truth must arrive.

Summary

The way to get a maximum rate of "economic growth"—assuming this to be our aim—is to give maximum encouragement to production, employment, saving, and investment. And the way to do this is to maintain a free market and a sound currency. It is to encourage profits, which must in turn encourage both investment and employment. It is to refrain from oppressive taxation that siphons away the funds that would otherwise be available for investment. It is to allow free wage rates that permit and encourage full employment. It is to allow free interest rates, which would tend to maximize saving and investment.

The way to *slow down* the rate of economic growth is, of course, precisely the opposite of this. It is to discourage production, employment, saving and investment by incessant interventions, controls, threats, and harassment. It is to frown upon profits, to declare that they are excessive, to file constant antitrust suits, to control prices by law or by threats, to levy confiscatory taxes that discourage new investment and siphon off the funds that make investment possible, to hold down interest rates artificially to the point where real saving is discouraged and malinvestment encouraged, to deprive employers of genuine freedom of bargaining, to grant excessive immunities and privileges to labor unions so that their demands are chronically excessive and chronically threaten unemployment—and then to try to offset all these policies by government spending, deficits, and monetary inflation. But I have just described precisely the policies that most of the fanatical Growthmen advocate.

Their recipe for inducing growth always turns out to be —inflation. This does lead to the *illusion* of growth, which is measured in their statistics in monetary terms. What the Growthmen do not realize is that the magic of inflation is always a short-run magic, and quickly played out. It can work temporarily and under special conditions—when it causes prices to rise faster than wages and so restores or expands profit margins. But this can happen only in the early stages of an inflation that is not expected to continue. And it can happen even then only because of the temporary acquiescence or passivity of the labor union leaders. The consequences of this short-lived paradise are malinvestment, waste, a wanton redistribution of wealth and income, the growth of speculation and gambling, immorality and corruption, disillusionment, social resentment, discontent, upheaval and riots, bankruptcy, increased governmental controls, and eventual collapse. This year's euphoria becomes next year's hangover. Sound long-run growth is always retarded.

Ultimately we must fall back upon an a priori conclusion, yet a conclusion that is confirmed by the whole range of human experience: that when each of us is free to work out his own economic destiny, within the framework of the market economy, the institution of private property, and the general rule of law, we will all improve our economic condition much faster than when we are ordered around by bureaucrats.

/\/\/\/\/\

CHAPTER 17

Government As
Prosperity-Maker

/\

IN A SPEECH IN DECEMBER, 1967, GILBERT W.
Fitzhugh, chairman of the board of the Metropolitan
Life Insurance Company, neatly stuck a pin in the pre-
tensions of "the new breed" of economists.

I shall risk ostracism [he said] by questioning the basic
premises of the thesis that government planners can fine-
tune the economy to such an extent as to assure steady
growth in employment and productivity . . . while at the
same time maintaining a sound dollar. These premises seem
to be:
1. Economists now have sufficiently accurate information to
predict whether the government should be pursuing expan-
sionary or restraining policies;

2. This informaton is available in time to be of practical use;

3. The fallible human beings who make the decisions for the government based on these data will make the right decision based on economics rather than politics; and

4. That these decisions will be made promptly at the right time.

Does recent history give us confidence that *any* of these four premises, much less *all* of them, will be met in this practical world of ours? On the contrary, is there not some reason to feel that government actions in recent years have been more unstabilizing than stabilizing?

Mr. Fitzhugh's doubts were not only justified, but understated.

One of the premises of the "new economists" is that the government bureaucrats in charge of "keeping the economy on an even keel" are not only capable of forecasting future business conditions (or forecasting what they would be in the absence of timely governmental intervention), but are capable of forecasting them consistently better than private business. In fact, a chairman of the Council of Economic Advisers once informed me that without him the American economy would be "flying blind."

One of the elementary facts that the would-be economic fine-tuners overlook is that most of the chief statistics on which they rely are not known until a month or two after the conditions they record. Even the latest statistics, in other words, only tell us what past conditions were, not what present conditions are, much less what they will be. And when some major economic event occurs—like the devaluation of the British pound by 14 per cent in November, 1967—our government economists, like the rest of us, don't know about it until after it happens.

The only way government bureaucrats know of keeping prosperity going is to inflate some more—to increase the deficit or to pump more money into the system.

They proudly claim credit for a good result. But when the inflation begins to get out of hand, when the deficit in the balance of payments mounts, when the integrity of the dollar is threatened, they disclaim all responsibility. They explain that it is politically impossible to cut back government spending and would precipitate a crisis to stop expanding the supply of paper money. The only remedy they suggest is to raise taxes still further to pay for their own past extravagances.

They denounce the banks for raising interest rates. They denounce business for raising prices and for investing abroad. In brief, they denounce private enterprise for the consequences of their own reckless policies and demand still more governmental controls.

/\/\/\/\/\

CHAPTER 18

Uruguay: Welfare State Gone Wild

/\

IF THERE WERE A NOBEL PRIZE FOR THE MOST EX-
treme or worst example of the welfare state (and if the
outright Communist states of Russia and China were
made ineligible), which country has done most to earn
it?

The decision would be a hard one. Among the outstanding candidates would be Britain, France, Sweden,
and India. But the British case, though the most familiar, is certainly not the worst; it is the most discussed
and most deplored because of the former eminence of
Britain in the world.

The tragedy certainly reaches its greatest dimensions
in India, with much of its 500 million population always
on the verge of famine, and kept there by an incredible

mixture of economic controls, planning, welfarism and socialism, imposed by its central and state governments. We have already discussed a few of India's sins of commission and omission in Chapter 9. However, India has always been a poverty-stricken country, periodically swept by drought or floods resulting in human misery on a catastrophic scale, and it is often difficult to calculate just how much worse off its governmental policies have made it.

Perhaps the most dramatic example of a country needlessly ruined by "welfare" policies is Uruguay. Here is a country only about a third larger than the state of Wisconsin, with a population of only about 2.8 million. Yet that population is predominantly of European origin, with a literacy rate estimated at 90 per cent. It was once so distinguished for its high living standards and good management that it was frequently referred to as "the Switzerland of Latin America."

Uruguay adopted an elaborate state pension system as early as 1919. But its major troubles seem to have begun after March, 1952, when the office of president was abolished, and Uruguay was governed by a nine-man national council elected for a four-year term, six members of which belonged to the majority party and three to the leading minority party. All nine were given equal power.

What is so discouraging about the example of Uruguay is not only that its welfare programs persisted, but that they became more extreme in spite of the successive disasters to which they led. The story seems so incredible that instead of telling it in my own words, I prefer to present it as a series of snapshots taken by different first-hand observers at intervals over the years.

The first snapshot I present is one taken by Karel Norsky in the *Manchester Guardian Weekly* of July 12, 1956:

Uruguay today offers the sad spectacle of a sick Welfare State. It is living in a Korean boomday dream. . . . No politician comes out with the home truth that this country's wide range of welfare services has to be paid for with funds which have to be earned. Demagogy is used as a sedative. The result is that the foreign payments deficit is increasing, internal debt soaring, wage demands accumulating, prices rising, and the Uruguayan peso rapidly depreciating. Nepotism is rife. Now one in every three citizens in Montevideo, which accounts for a third of the country's 3 million inhabitants, is a public servant, draws a small salary, is supposed to work half a day in a Government office, and more often than not spends the rest of his time doing at least one other job in a private enterprise. . . . Corruption is by no means absent. . . .

The foreign payments deficit has been running at a monthly rate of about 5 million pesos. The public servants are asking for a substantial increase in salaries. The meat-packing workers are on strike for higher pay and a "guaranteed" amount of a daily ration of four pounds of meat well below market price. . . .

No politician here can hope to get a majority by advocating austerity, harder work, and the sacrifice of even some of the Welfare State features.

I should like to pause here to underline this last paragraph, for it illustrates what is perhaps the most ominous aspect of the welfare state everywhere. This is that once a subsidy, pension, or benefit payment is extended to any group, it is immediately regarded as a "right." No matter what the crisis facing the budget or the currency, it becomes "politically impossible" to discontinue or reduce it. We will find this repeatedly illustrated in Uruguay.

The next snapshot I present was taken by S. J. Rundt & Associates of New York nearly seven years later, in April, 1963:

In one of his first statements the new President of the National Council admitted that Uruguay is practically bankrupt. . . . He made it pretty clear, however, that the country's welfare system of long standing will remain more or less unchanged.

The "social laboratory of the Americas," Uruguay has launched a legislative program which goes much further toward the complete "welfare state" than any similar plan in this hemisphere. . . . The government grants family allowances based on the number of children; employees cannot be dismissed without proper indemnification; both men and women vote at the age of 18. . . .

An elaborate and all-encompassing state pension system was introduced as early as 1919. Financed by payroll deductions of 14 to 17 per cent, which must be matched by employers, a pension is available to any Uruguayan at the age of 55 after 30 years of work, or at 60 after 10 years. At retirement, the worker draws his highest salary, plus what has been deducted for pensions. . . . Employees obtain free medical service and are entitled to 20 days of annual vacation with pay. The government takes care of expectant and nursing mothers.

The overwhelming expenses of a super-welfare state (where nearly one-fifth of the population is dependent on government salaries) and the uncertain income from a predominantly livestock and agricultural economy have left their marks. Today, Uruguay is in severe financial and fiscal stress. . . .

Inflation is rampant. . . . Local production has declined sharply. Unemployment has risen. There are many severe strikes. Income from tourism has fallen off markedly. . . .

So far as exchange controls and import restrictions are concerned, Uruguay has tried them all. . . .

In an effort to prevent another buying spree in 1963, the new Administration decreed an import ban for 90 days on a wide array of goods considered non-essential. . . . All told, the ban applies to about one-third of all Uruguayan importations. . . . The smuggling of goods, mainly from Brazil and

Argentina, has become one of the foremost headaches of
Montevideo planners. . . .

Capital flight during 1963 is estimated at between $40 million and $50 million. . . .

The budget deficit in 1961 nearly doubled to 210 million
pesos. The situation turned from bad to worse in 1962 when
the Treasury recorded the largest deficit in 30 years. . . .
Press reports cite a red figure of 807 million pesos. The Treasury is said to owe by now nearly 700 million pesos to the
pension funds and roughly a billion pesos to Banco de la
República. The salaries of public officials are at least one
month behind schedule. . . .

Labor costs in Uruguay, the Western Hemisphere's foremost welfare state, are high. The many contributions toward
various social benefits—retirement, family allotments, sickness, maternity, accident, and unemployment insurance—
vary from industry to industry, but the general average for
industry as a whole is at least 50 per cent of the payroll. In
some sectors, the percentage is much higher. . . .

Social unrest is rising. . . . Widespread and costly strikes
have become the order of the day. As a rule, they involve
demands for pay hikes, sometimes as high as 50 per cent.

Our third snapshot was taken by Sterling G. Slappey
in *Nation's Business* magazine four years later, in April,
1967:

Montevideo—Two hundred imported buses are rusting
away on an open dock while Uruguayan government bureaucrats bicker with each other over payment of port charges.
The buses have not moved in nearly four years.

Scores of men listed under false female names receive
regular government handouts through Uruguay's socialized
hospitals. They are listed as "wet nurses."

At many government offices there are twice as many public
servants as there are desks and chairs. The trick is to get to
work early so you won't have to stand during the four to six

hour workday that Uruguayan bureaucrats enjoy.

It is rather common for government workers to retire on full pay at 45. It is equally common to collect on one retirement while holding a second job or to hold a job while collecting unemployment compensation. These are a few of the facts of life in Uruguay—a nation gone wild over the welfare state. . . .

Between 40 and 45 per cent of the 2.6 million people in this once affluent land are now dependent on the government for their total income. These include youthful "pensioners" who have no great problem getting themselves fired or declared redundant, thereby qualifying for large retirement benefits. . . .

At any given moment eight to ten strikes are going on, in a nation which until fifteen years ago called itself "the Switzerland of Latin America" because its people were so industrious, busy and neat. Montevideo is now one of the world's filthiest cities outside the Orient. The people have so little pride left they litter their streets with paper and dump their nastiest garbage on the curb. . . .

Besides controlling meat and wool production and supplying meat to Montevideo, the government also entirely operates:

Fishing; seal catching; alcohol production; life and accident insurance; the PTT—post office, telephone and telegraph; petroleum and kerosene industry; airlines; railroads; tug boats; gambling casinos; lotteries; theaters; most hospitals; television and radio channels; three official banks; the largest transit company. . . .

In 1950 the Uruguayan peso, South America's most solid coin, was worth 50 cents. During a six-day period last February, the value of the peso slumped from 72 to the $1 to 77.

Cost of living went up 88 per cent in 1965. During 1966 the increase was something like 40 to 50 per cent.

To keep pace the government has increased its spending, ground out more paper money and lavishly passed out huge pay raises—some as high as 60 per cent a year. . . .

One fiscal expert diagnoses Uruguay's troubles as "English sickness" which, he says, means trying to get as much as possible out of the community while contributing as little as possible towards it.

Until President Gestido took over, Uruguay had been ruled for fifteen years by a nine-member council in a collegiate system of government. It was idealistic, unworkable and rather silly from the start. It quickly fragmented, making the government a coalition of seven different groups. Every year a different member of the council took over as president, or council chief.

The collegiate system was a Tammany Hall patronage-type of group. Instead of each party watching the opposition, all took care of their friends and got their cousins government sinecures.

The western world has rarely seen such patronage, nepotism, favoritism.

The return to a presidential system brought hopes that Uruguay's extreme welfarism could now be mitigated. But here is our fourth snapshot, taken by C. L. Sulzberger for the New York *Times* of October 11, 1967:

Montevideo—Contemporary England or Scandinavia might well take a long southwesterly look at Uruguay while murmuring: "There but for the grace of God go I." For Uruguay is the welfare state gone wild, and this fact, at last acknowledged by the government, brought about today's political crisis and the declaration of a state of emergency.

This is the only country in the Western Hemisphere where the kind of democratic socialism practiced in Norway, Labor Britain or New Zealand has been attempted. Alas, thanks to warped conceptions and biased application, the entire social and economic structure has been set askew. Here charity begins at home. One out of three adults receives some kind of pension. Forty per cent of the labor force is employed by the state. Political parties compete to expand a ridiculously swollen bureaucracy which only works a thirty-hour week. . . .

The cost of living has multiplied 32 times in the past

decade. Gross national production has actually declined 9 per cent and this year will take a nose dive. . . .

Instead of having one President, like the Swiss they elected a committee and, not being Swiss, the Uruguayans saw to it the committee couldn't run the country. The result was a system of self-paralysis. . . .

Anyone can retire on full salary after thirty years on the job, but with full salary worth one thirty-second of its worth ten years ago, the pension isn't very helpful. To compound the confusion, trade unions make a habit of striking. Right now the bank employes refuse to handle government checks so neither wage-earners nor pension-receivers get paid. . . .

This was a needless tragedy. Uruguay has proportionately more literacy and more doctors than the United States. It is underpopulated and has a well-developed middle class. . . .

Uruguay should serve as a warning to other welfare states.

Our fifth snapshot was taken by S. J. Rundt & Associates on August 6, 1968:

The mess continues . . . and seems to perpetuate itself. . . . The government is getting tougher and Uruguayans more obstreperous. The powerful and sharply leftist, Communist-led 400,000 member CNT (National Workers Convention) is on and off 24-hour work stoppages in protest against the lid clamped on pay boosts by the price, wage and dividend freeze decreed on June 28. . . . The currently severe six-month drought has brought a gloomy brownout, after a 50 per cent reduction in electric power use was decreed. . . . The near-darkness helps sporadic anti-government rioting and terrorist activities. A leading pro-government radio transmitter was destroyed by bombs. . . . Last year there were 500 strikes; the dismal record will surely be broken in 1968. . . .

Of a population of around 2.6 million, the number of gainfully active Uruguayans is at the most 900,000. Pensioners number in excess of 300,000. Months ago the unemployed came to 250,000, or almost 28 per cent of the work force, and the figure must now be higher. . . .

The government closed at least three supermarkets and many stores for having upped prices, as well as such institutions as private hospitals that had violated the wage-price freeze decree. But despite rigid press censorship and Draconian anti-riot and anti-strike ukases, threatening punishment by military tribunals, calm fails to return.

Our sixth and final snapshot of a continuing crisis is from a New York *Times* dispatch of January 21, 1969:

Striking Government employes rioted in downtown Montevideo today, smashing windows, setting up flaming barricades and sending tourists fleeing in panic. The police reported that one person had been killed and 32 injured.

The demonstrators acted in groups of 30 to 50, racing through a 30-block area, snarling traffic with their barricades, and attacking buses and automobiles. The police fought back with tear gas, high-pressure water hoses and clubs. ...

The striking civil servants were demanding payment of monthly salary bonuses of $24, which they say is two months overdue.

These six snapshots, taken at different intervals over a period of thirteen years, involve considerable repetition; but the repetition is part of the point. The obvious reforms were never made.

Here are a few salient statistics to show what was happening between the snapshots:

In 1965 consumer prices increased 88 per cent over those in the preceding year. In 1966 they increased 49 per cent over 1965. In 1967 they increased 136 per cent over 1966. By August, 1968, they had increased 61 per cent over 1967.

The average annual commercial rate of interest was 36 per cent in 1965. In 1966, 1967, and August, 1968, it ranged between 32 and 50 per cent.

The volume of money increased from 2,924 million

pesos in 1961 to 10,509 in 1965, 13,458 in 1966, 30,163 in 1967, and 40,738 million pesos in August, 1968.

In 1961 there were 11 pesos to the American dollar. In 1965 there were 60; in 1966 there were 70; in early 1967 there were 86; at the end of 1967 there were 200, and in April, 1968, there were 250.

Uruguay's warning to the United States, and to the world, is that governmental welfarism, with its ever-increasing army of pensioners and other beneficiaries, is fatally easy to launch and fatally easy to extend, but almost impossible to bring to a halt—and quite impossible politically to reverse, no matter how obvious and catastrophic its consequences become. It leads to runaway inflation, to state bankruptcy, to political disorder and disintegration, and finally to repressive dictatorship. Yet no country ever seems to learn from the example of another.

‏‏‎ ‎.‏‏‎ ‎٨.٨.٨.٨.٨.٨

Inflation Is Worldwide

٨.٨

THE EPIDEMIC OF INFLATION IS NOT MERELY AMERI-
can but worldwide. And in most countries it is growing
more virulent.

The First National City Bank of New York keeps
score annually. Its table published in August, 1968,
shows the currency depreciation in 45 countries, in
1967 and over the preceding 10 years, as measured by
cost-of-living indices.

The table shows that in every one of the 45 countries
the purchasing power of the monetary unit declined in
the 10-year period 1957-67, and that the rate of decline
in the value of money in 1967 exceeded the 10-year
average in 27 of those countries. The median rate of
depreciation in the 45 countries in 1967 was 3.8 per

cent, compared with a median rate of 3.3 per cent a year for the decade as a whole.

The buying power of the United States dollar suffered a rate of shrinkage of 2.7 per cent in 1967, compared with an average rate of 1.7 per cent a year over the past decade. (The dollar's purchasing power shrank by 4.0 per cent during 1968.)

At the end of 1967 the United States dollar bought only 84 per cent as much as it bought 10 years before. On the same 10-year basis of comparison Canada's currency bought only 82 per cent as much, Belgium's 80, West Germany's 79, Switzerland's 76, the United Kingdom's 75, Holland's 73, Italy's 71, Sweden's 69, Japan's 66, France's 62, India's 54, Spain's 50, Vietnam's 31, Chile's 11, Argentina's 6, and Brazil's only 2 per cent as much.

The three countries with the worst records were Latin American countries; but so, remarkably, were the three countries with the best records. These were Guatemala, whose currency in 1967 still bought 99 per cent as much as it did 10 years before; El Salvador, whose currency bought 94 per cent as much; and Venezuela, whose currency bought 88 per cent as much.

This contrast shows that the extent of inflation has nothing to do with the wealth or resources of a country. It is certainly not the result of a "scarcity of goods." It is true that Argentina and Brazil are not outstandingly rich countries, but the nations that suffered from inflation least, Guatemala and El Salvador, are among the poorest in the world.

The truth is that inflation is always the result of governmental policy. It is a consequence of printing too much money.

If the Citibank's table had compared not only the extent of the fall in buying power of each of the 45

countries' currencies, but also the respective increases
in the amount of money issued by each country, this
fact would have been made clear. Digging these comparisons out myself from the monthly publication of the
International Monetary Fund, *International Monetary
Statistics*, I find that in Guatemala, for example, the
supply of currency was increased from 120 million quet-
zales in 1957 to 157 million in 1967, a rise of only 31 per
cent. In Brazil, by contrast, the supply of money was
increased from 291 million new cruzeiros in 1957 to
19,593 million in 1967, a rise of 6,633 per cent. This is
sufficient explanation of the fact that the Guatemalan
currency lost only 1 per cent of its purchasing power in
the 10-year period while the Brazilian currency lost 98
per cent of its former purchasing power. Similar comparisons could be made for the other countries.

The governments that have done most to expand
their issuance of money have done so, or have "had" to
do so, because they plunged into welfare schemes and
socialistic programs that brought on enormous chronic
budget deficits.

In their rush to bring perpetual prosperity and to
"end poverty" in their own lands they have eroded the
value of their own people's savings and left millions of
their most hard-working and thrifty citizens facing the
specter of poverty.

/\/\/\/\

CHAPTER 20

The Case for the Gold Standard

IN FEBRUARY OF 1965 PRESIDENT DE GAULLE OF
France startled the financial world by calling for a return to an international gold standard. American and
British monetary managers replied that he was asking
for the restoration of a world lost forever. But some
eminent economists strongly endorsed his proposal.
They argued that only a return to national currencies
directly convertible into gold could bring an end to the
chronic monetary inflation of the last twenty years in
nearly every country in the world.

What is the gold standard? How did it come about?
When and why was it abandoned? And why is there
now in many quarters a strong demand for its restoration? We can best understand the answers to these
questions by a glance into history.

In primitive societies exchange was conducted by barter. But as labor and production became more divided and specialized, a man found it hard to find someone who happened to have just what he wanted and happened to want just what he had. So people tried to exchange their goods first for some article that nearly everybody wanted, so that they could exchange this article in turn for the exact things they happened to want.

This common commodity became a medium of exchange—money.

All sorts of things have been used in human history as such a common medium of exchange—cattle, tobacco, precious stones, the precious metals, particularly silver and gold. Finally gold became dominant, the "standard" money.

Gold had tremendous advantages. It could be fashioned into beautiful ornaments and jewelry. Because it was both beautiful and scarce, gold combined very high value with comparatively little weight and bulk; it could therefore he easily held and stored. Gold "kept" indefinitely; it did not spoil or rust; it was not only durable but practically indestructible. Gold could be hammered or stamped into almost any shape or precisely divided into any desired size or unit of weight. There were chemical and other tests that could establish whether it was genuine. And as it could be stamped into coins of a precise weight, the values of all other goods could be exactly expressed in units of gold. It therefore became not only the medium of exchange but the "standard of value." Records show that gold was being used as a form of money as long ago as 3,000 B.C. Gold coins were struck as early as 800 or 700 B.C.

One of gold's very advantages, however, also presented a problem. Its high value compared with its weight and bulk increased the risks of its being stolen.

In the sixteenth and even into the nineteenth century (as one will find from the plays of Ben Jonson and Molière and the novels of George Eliot and Balzac) some people kept almost their entire fortunes in gold in their own houses. But most people came more and more into the habit of leaving their gold for safekeeping in the vaults of goldsmiths. The goldsmiths gave them a receipt for it.

The Origin of Banks

Then came a development that probably no one had originally foreseen. The people who had left their gold in a goldsmith's vault found, when they wanted to make a purchase or pay a debt, that they did not have to go to the vaults themselves for their gold. They could simply issue an order to the goldsmith to pay over the gold to the person from whom they had purchased something. This second man might find in turn that he did not want the actual gold; he was content to leave it for safekeeping at the goldsmith's, and in turn issue orders to the goldsmith to pay specified amounts of gold to still a third person. And so on.

This was the origin of banks, and of both bank notes and checks. If the receipts were made out by the goldsmith or banker himself, for round sums payable to bearer, they were bank notes. If they were orders to pay made out by the legal owners of the gold themselves, for varying specified amounts to be paid to particular persons, they were checks. In either case, though the ownership of the gold constantly changed and the bank notes circulated, the gold itself almost never left the vault!

When the goldsmiths and banks made the discovery that their customers rarely demanded the actual gold, they came to feel that it was safe to issue more notes promising to pay gold than the actual amount of gold they had on hand. They counted on the high unlikelihood that everybody would demand his gold at once.

This practice seemed safe and even prudent for another reason. An honest bank did not simply issue more notes, more IOU's, than the amount of actual gold it had in its vaults. It would make loans to borrowers secured by salable assets of the borrowers. The bank notes issued in excess of the gold held by the bank were also secured by these assets. An honest bank's assets therefore continued to remain at least equal to its liabilities.

There was one catch. The bank's liabilities, which were in gold, were all payable *on demand,* without prior notice. But its assets, consisting mainly of its loans to customers, were most of them payable only on some date in the future. The bank might be "solvent" (in the sense that the value of its assets equaled the value of its liabilities) but it would be at least partly "illiquid." If all its depositors demanded their gold at once, it could not possibly pay them all.

Yet such a situation might not develop in a lifetime. So in nearly every country the banks went on expanding their credit until the amount of bank-note and demand-deposit liabilities (that is, the amount of "money") was several times the amount of gold held in the banks' vaults.

The Fractional Reserve

In the United States in mid-1969 there were $19 of Federal Reserve notes and demand-deposit liabilities— i.e., $19 of money—for every $1 of gold.

Up until 1929, this situation—a gold standard with only a "fractional" gold reserve—was accepted as sound by the great body of monetary economists, and even as the best system attainable. There were two things about it, however, that were commonly overlooked. First, if there was, say, four, five, or ten times as much note and deposit "money" in circulation as the amount of gold against which this money had been issued, it meant that prices were far higher as a result of this more abundant money, perhaps four, five, or ten times higher, than if there had been no more money than the amount of gold. And business was built upon, and had become dependent upon, this amount of money and this level of wages and prices.

Now if, in this situation, some big bank or company failed, or the prices of stocks tumbled, or some other event precipitated a collapse of confidence, prices of commodities might begin to fall; more failures would be touched off; banks would refuse to renew loans; they would start calling old loans; goods would be dumped on the market. As the amount of loans was contracted, the amount of bank notes and deposits against them would also shrink. In short, the supply of money itself would begin to fall. This would touch off a still further decline of prices and buying and a further decline of confidence.

That is the story of every major depression. It is the story of the Great Depression from 1929 to 1933.

From Boom to Slump

What happened in 1929 and after, some economists argue, is that the gold standard "collapsed." They say we should never go back to it or depend upon it again. But other economists argue that it was not the gold

standard that "collapsed" but unsound political and
economic policies that destroyed it. Excessive expansion of credit, they say, is bound to lead in the end to
a violent contraction of credit. A boom stimulated by
easy credit and cheap money must be followed by a
crisis and a slump.

In 1944, however, at a conference in Bretton Woods,
New Hampshire, the official representatives of 44 nations decided—mainly under the influence of John
Maynard Keynes of Great Britain and Harry Dexter
White of the United States—to set up a new international currency system in which the central banks of the
leading countries would cooperate with each other and
coordinate their currency systems through an International Monetary Fund. They would all deposit "quotas"
in the Fund, only one-quarter of which need be in gold,
and the rest in their own currencies. They would all be
entitled to draw on this Fund quickly for credits and
other currencies.

The United States alone explicitly undertook to keep
its currency convertible at all times into gold. This privilege of converting their dollars was not given to its own
citizens, who were forbidden to hold gold (except in
the form of jewelry or teeth fillings); the privilege was
given only to foreign central banks and official international institutions. Our government pledged itself to
convert these foreign holdings of dollars into gold on
demand at the fixed rate of $35 an ounce. Two-way
convertibility at this rate meant that a dollar was the
equivalent of one thirty-fifth of an ounce of gold.

The other currencies were not tied to gold in this
direct way. They were simply tied to the dollar by the
commitment of the various countries not to let their
currencies fluctuate (in terms of the dollar) by more
than 1 per cent either way from their adopted par values. The other countries could hold and count dollars as

part of their reserves on the same basis as if dollars were gold.

The IMF Promotes Inflation

The system has not worked well. There is no evidence that it has "shortened the duration and lessened the degree of disequilibrium in the international balances of payments of members," which was one of its six principal declared purposes. It has not maintained a stable value and purchasing power of the currencies of individual members. This vital need was not even a declared purpose.

In fact, under it inflation and depreciation of currencies have been rampant. Of the 48 or so national members of the Fund in 1949, practically all except the United States devalued their currencies (i.e., reduced their value) that year, following devaluation of the British pound from $4.03 to $2.80. Of the 111 present members of the Fund, the great majority have either formally devalued since they joined, or allowed their currencies to fall in value since then as compared with the dollar.

The dollar itself, since 1944, has lost 50 per cent of its purchasing power. In just the ten years ending in 1967 (as we saw in the last chapter) the German mark lost 21 per cent of its purchasing power, the British pound 25 per cent, the Italian lira 29 per cent, the French franc 38 per cent, and leading South American currencies from 94 to 98 per cent.

In addition, the two "key" currencies, the currencies that can be used as reserves by other countries—the British pound sterling and the dollar—have been plagued by special problems. The pound was devalued from $4.03 to $2.80 in 1949 and from $2.80 to $2.40 in

1967, and yet has had to be repeatedly rescued by huge loans from the United States, from the Fund, and from a consortium of countries.

Balance of Payments

The United States has been harassed since the end of 1957 by a serious and apparently chronic "deficit in the balance of payments." This is the name given to the excess in the amount of dollars going abroad (for foreign aid, for investments, for tourist expenditures, for imports, and for other payments) over the amount of dollars coming in (in payment for our exports to foreign countries, etc.). This deficit in the balance of payments has been running since the er d of 1957 at a rate of more than $2.8 billion a year. At the end of 1968, the total deficit in our balance of payments came to some $30 billion.

This had led, among other things, to a fall in the amount of gold holdings of the United States from $22.9 billion at the end of 1957 to $10.4 billion in mid-1969.

Other changes have taken place. As a result of the chronic deficit in the balance of payments, foreigners have short-term claims on the United States of $37.8 billion. And $13.4 billion of these are held by foreign central banks and international organizations that have a direct legal right to demand gold for them. The remaining $24.4 billion are an indirect claim on our gold.

This is why officials and economists not only in the United States but all over the Western world are now discussing a world monetary reform. Most of them are putting forward proposals to increase "reserves" and to increase "liquidity." They argue that there isn't enough "liquidity"—that is, that there isn't enough money and credit, or soon won't be—to conduct the constantly

growing volume of world trade. Most of them tell us that
the gold standard is outmoded. In any case, they say,
there isn't enough gold in the world to serve as the basis
for national currencies and international settlements.

The Minority View

But the advocates of a return to a full gold standard,
who though now in a minority include some of the
world's most distinguished economists, are not impressed by these arguments for still further monetary
expansion. They say these are merely arguments for still
further inflation. And they contend that this further
monetary expansion or inflation, apart from its positive
dangers, would be a futile means even of achieving the
ends that the expansionists themselves have in mind.

Suppose, say the gold-standard advocates, we were
to double the amount of money now in the world. We
could not, in the long run, conduct any greater volume
of business and trade than we could before. For the
result of increasing the amount of money would be
merely to increase correspondingly the wages and
prices at which business and trade were conducted. In
other words, the result of doubling the supply of money,
other things remaining unchanged, would be roughly to
cut in half the purchasing power of the currency unit.
The process would be as ridiculous as it would be futile.
This is the sad lesson that inflating countries soon or late
learn to their sorrow.

The Great Merit of Gold

The detractors of gold complain that it is difficult and
costly to increase the supply of the metal, and that this
depends upon the "accidents" of discovery of new

mines or the invention of better processes of extraction. But the advocates of a gold standard argue that this is precisely gold's great merit. The supply of gold is governed by nature; it is not, like the supply of paper money, subject merely to the schemes of demagogues or the whims of politicians. Nobody ever thinks he has quite enough money. Once the idea is accepted that money is something whose supply is determined simply by the printing press, it becomes impossible for the politicians in power to resist the constant demands for further inflation. Gold may not be a theoretically perfect basis for money; but it has the merit of making the money supply, and therefore the value of the monetary unit, independent of governmental manipulation and political pressure.

And this is a tremendous merit. When a country is not on a gold standard, when its citizens are not even permitted to own gold, when they are told that irredeemable paper money is just as good, when they are compelled to accept payment in such paper of debts or pensions that are owed to them, when what they have put aside, for retirement or old age, in savings banks or insurance policies, consists of this irredeemable paper money, then they are left without protection as the issue of this paper money is increased and the purchasing power of each unit falls; then they can be completely impoverished by the political decisions of the "monetary managers."

I have just said that the dollar itself, "the best currency in the world," has lost 50 per cent of its purchasing power of 24 years ago. This means that a man who retired with $10,000 of savings in 1944 now finds that that capital will buy only half as much as it did then.

But Americans, so far, have been the very lucky ones. The situation is much worse in England, and still worse in France. In some South American countries practically the whole value of people's savings—94 to 98 cents in every dollar—has been wiped out in the last ten years.

Not a Managed Money

The tremendous merit of gold is, if we want to put it that way, a negative one: It is *not* a managed paper money that can ruin everyone who is legally forced to accept it or who puts his confidence in it. The technical criticisms of the gold standard become utterly trivial when compared with this single merit. The experience of the last twenty years in practically every country proves that the monetary managers are the pawns of the politicians, and cannot be trusted.

Many people, including economists who ought to know better, talk as if the world had already abandoned the gold standard. They are mistaken. The world's currencies are still tied to gold, though in a loose, indirect, and precarious way. Other currencies are tied to the American dollar, and convertible into it, at definite "official" rates (unfortunately subject to sudden change) through the International Monetary Fund. And the dollar is still, though in an increasingly nominal way, convertible into gold at $35 an ounce.

Indeed, the American problem today, and the world problem today, is precisely how to maintain this limited convertibility of the dollar (and hence indirectly of other currencies) into a fixed quantity of gold.

The $35 Question

The crucial question that the world has now to answer is this: As the present system and present policies are rapidly becoming untenable, shall the world's cur-

rencies abandon all links to gold, and leave the supply
of each nation's money to be determined by political
management, or shall the world's leading currencies
return to a gold standard—that is, shall each leading
currency be made once again fully convertible into gold
on demand at a fixed rate?

Whatever may have been the shortcomings of the old
gold standard, as it operated in the nineteenth and the
early twentieth century, it gave the world, in fact, an
international money. When all leading currencies were
directly convertible into a fixed amount of gold on demand, they were of course at all times convertible into
each other at the equivalent fixed cross rates. Businessmen in every country could have confidence in the
currencies of other countries. In final settlement, gold
was the one universally acceptable currency everywhere. It is still the one universally acceptable commodity to those who are still legally allowed to get it.

Instead of ignoring or deploring or combating this
fact, the world's governments might start building on it
once more.

/\\/\\/\\/\\

CHAPTER 21

The Fallacy of Foreign Aid

/\\

THE ADVOCATES OF FOREIGN AID BELIEVE THAT IT helps not only the country that gets it but the country that gives it. They believe, therefore, that it promotes worldwide "economic growth." They are mistaken in these assumptions.

I should make clear at the beginning that when I refer here to foreign aid I mean government-to-government aid. Still more specifically, I mean government-to-government "economic" aid. I am not considering here intergovernmental military aid extended either in wartime or peacetime. The justification of military aid will depend, in each case, only partly on economic considerations, and mainly on a complex set of political and military factors.

It ought to be clear, to begin with, that foreign aid retards the economic growth and the capital development of the country that grants it. If it is fully paid for out of taxes at the time it is granted, it puts an additional tax burden on industry and reduces incentives at the same time that it takes funds that would otherwise have gone into new domestic investment. If it is not fully paid for, but financed out of budget deficits, it brings all the evils of inflation. It leads to rising prices and costs. It leads to deficits in the balance of payments, to a loss of gold, and to loss of confidence in the soundness of the currency unit. In either case foreign aid must set back the donor country's capital development.

All the consequences just described have occurred in the United States. In the 23 years ending June 30, 1968, American foreign aid—grants, loans, and interest—reached the stupendous total of $171 billion. As the public debt increased from $259 billion at the end of fiscal 1945 to $359 billion in 1968, this means that $100 billion of this foreign aid was in effect paid for by borrowing and by inflating the currency, and $71 billion by added taxation. Without the foreign aid handouts we could have avoided both the inflation and the added taxation. We could have avoided both the cumulative deficit of $30 billion in the balance of payments and the loss of $10 billion gold in those years. Today, American "liberals" are talking about all the billions we ought or will need to spend to extend and improve our roads and highways, to improve and increase our housing and to rehabilitate our blighted cities, to combat air pollution and water pollution, to bring more water to the cities and to turn salt water into fresh. The $171 billion that went into foreign aid would have covered practically all the improvements in this direction that most of these "liberals" are demanding.

The Pump-Priming Argument

We sometimes hear it said by American advocates of foreign aid (and we very frequently hear it said by many of the foreign recipients of our aid, and *always* by the Communists) that the United States has got great economic advantages out of its foreign aid program. We desperately need "outlets" and "new markets" for our "surplus." We must give part of our goods away, or give foreigners the dollars with which to buy them, to keep our factories going and to maintain full employment. This program was even necessary, according to the Communists, to "postpone the inevitable collapse" of capitalism.

It should not be necessary to point out that this whole argument is unmitigated nonsense. If it were true that we could create prosperity and full employment by making goods to give away, then we would not have to give them to foreign countries. We could accomplish the same result by making the goods to dump into the sea. Or, far better, our government could give the money or the goods to our own poor.

It ought to be clear even to the feeblest intelligence that nobody can get rich by giving his goods away or making more goods to give away. What seems to confuse some otherwise clearheaded people when this proposition is applied to a nation rather than an individual is that it is possible for particular firms and persons within the nation to profit by such a transaction at the expense of the rest. The firms, for example, that are engaged in making the exported foreign aid commodities are paid for them by the aid-receiving country or by the United States Government. But the latter gets the money, in turn, from the American taxpayers. The taxpayers are poorer by the amount taken. If they had been allowed to keep it, they would have used it them-

selves to buy the goods they wanted. True, these would
not have been precisely the *same* goods as those that
were made and exported through the foreign aid program. But they would have supplied just as much employment. And Americans, rather than foreigners,
would have got what was made by this employment.

Buying Friends

"Yes," it may be conceded, "all of this may be true;
but let us not look at the matter so selfishly, or at least
not so nearsightedly. Think of the great blessings that
we have brought to the aid-receiving countries, and
think of the long-run political and other intangible
gains to the United States. We have prevented the aid-
receiving countries from going Communist, and the
continuance of our aid is necessary to continue to keep
them from going Communist. We have made the recipient countries our grateful allies and friends, and the
continuance of our foreign aid is necessary to continue
to keep them our grateful allies and friends."

First, let us look at these alleged intangible gains to
the United States. We are here admittedly in the realm
of opinion, in the realm of might-have-beens and
might-be's, where proof either way is hardly possible.
But there is no convincing evidence that any of our
aid-recipients that have *not* gone Communist *would*
have done so if they had not got our economic aid.
Communist Party membership in aid-receiving France
and Italy did not fall off; in fact it has shown a tendency
to increase in both countries with increasing prosperity.
And Cuba, the one country in the Western Hemisphere
that *has* gone Communist, did so in 1959 in spite of
having shared freely in our foreign aid in the preceding
twelve years. Cuba had been favored by us, in fact,

beyond all other countries in sugar import quotas and other indirect forms of economic help.

As for gaining grateful allies or even friends, there is no evidence that our $11 billion of lend-lease to Russia in World War II endeared us to the Russian leaders; that our aid to Poland, Yugoslavia, Indonesia, and Egypt turned Gomulka, Tito, Sukarno, or Nasser into dependable allies; that it has made France, or India, Mexico, Chile, Laos, Cambodia, Bolivia, Peru, Ghana, Panama, Algeria, and scores of other nations that have got our aid, into our grateful friends.

On the other hand, there *is* good reason to suspect that our aid has often had the opposite effect. Countries have found that whenever they look as if they are in danger of going Communist they get *more* American aid. This veiled threat becomes a recognized way of extorting more aid. And the leaders of governments getting our aid find it necessary to insult and denounce the United States to prove to their own followers that they are "independent" and not the "puppets" of "American imperialism." It is nearly always the United States embassies and information offices that periodically get rocks thrown through their windows, not the embassies of countries that have never given a cent.

Humanitarian Motives

"Still," it may be (and is) objected, "to mention any of these things is to take a shortsighted and selfish point of view. We should give foreign aid for purely humanitarian reasons. This will enable the poor nations to conquer their poverty, which they cannot do without our help. And when they have done so, we will have the reward of the charitable deed itself. Whether the recipients are grateful to us or not, our generosity will

redound in the long run to our own self-interest. A
world half rich and half poor is an unsafe world; it
breeds envy, hatred, and war. A fully prosperous world
is a world of peace and good will. Rich nations are
obviously better customers than poor nations. As the
underdeveloped nations develop, American foreign
trade and prosperity must also increase."

The final part of this argument is beyond dispute. It
is to America's long-run interest that all other countries
should be rich and productive, good customers, and
good sources of supply. What is wrong with the argument is the assumption that government-to-government aid is the way to bring about this desired
consummation.

The quickest and surest way to production, prosperity, and economic growth is through private enterprise.
The best way for governments to encourage private
enterprise is to establish justice, to enforce contracts, to
insure domestic peace and tranquility, to protect private property, and to secure the blessings of liberty,
including economic liberty—which means to stop putting obstacles in the way of private enterprise. If every
man is free to earn and to keep the fruits of his labor,
his incentives to work and to save, to invent and invest,
to launch new ventures, to try to build a better mouse-
trap than his neighbor, will be maximized. The effort of
each will bring the prosperity of all.

Under such a system more and more citizens will
acquire the capital to lend and invest, and will have the
maximum inducement to lend and invest at home. Very
quickly more and more foreigners will also notice the
investment opportunities in (let us call it) Libertania,
and their money will come in to speed its development.
They will place their funds where they promise to earn
the highest returns consonant with safety. This means
that the funds will go, if the investments are wisely

chosen, where they are most productive. They will go where they will produce the goods and services most wanted by productive Libertanians or by foreigners. In the latter case they will produce the maximum exports, or "foreign exchange," either to pay off the investment or to pay for the import of the foreign goods most needed.

The surest way for a poor nation to *stay* poor, on the other hand, is to harass, hobble, and straitjacket private enterprise or to discourage or destroy it by subsidized government competition, oppressive taxation, or outright expropriation.

Socialism versus Capitalism

Now government-to-government aid rests on socialistic assumptions and promotes socialism and stagnation, whereas private foreign investment rests on capitalistic assumptions and promotes private enterprise and maximum economic growth.

The egalitarian and socialistic assumptions underlying government-to-government aid are clear. Its main assumption is that the quickest way to "social" justice and progress is to take from the rich and give to the poor, to seize from Peter and give to Paul. The donor government seizes the aid money from its supposedly overrich taxpayers; it gives it to the receiving nation on the assumption that the latter "needs" the money—not on the assumption that it will make the most productive use of the money.

From the very beginning government-to-government aid has been on the horns of this dilemma. If on the one hand it is made without conditions, the funds are squandered and dissipated and fail to accomplish their purpose. But if the donor government attempts to impose conditions, its attempt is immediately resented. It is called "interfering in the internal affairs" of the recipient nation, which demands "aid without strings."

In the more than twenty expensive years that the foreign aid program has been in effect, American officials have swung uncertainly from one horn of this dilemma to the other—imposing conditions, dropping them when criticized, silently watching the aid funds being misused, then trying to impose conditions again. But recently American officials seemed bent on following the worst possible policy—that of imposing conditions, but exactly the wrong conditions.

In 1965 President Johnson announced that our future foreign aid would go to those countries "willing not only to talk about basic social change but who will act immediately on these reforms." But what our aid officials appeared to have in mind by "basic social change" was to ask of the countries that receive our grants, not that they give guarantees of the security of property, the integrity of their currencies, abstention from crippling government controls, and encouragement to free markets and free enterprise, but that they move in the direction of government planning, the paternalistic state, the redistribution of land, and other share-the-wealth schemes.

Land Reform Measures

The so-called "land reform" that our government officials often demanded meant destroying existing large-scale agricultural enterprises, dividing land into plots too small for efficient or economic cultivation, turning them over to untried managers, undermining the principles of private property, and opening a Pandora's box of still more radical demands.

Socialism and welfare programs lead to huge chronic government deficits and runaway inflation. This is what has happened in Latin America. In the ten years to the end of 1968 the currency of the Argentine lost 93 per cent of its purchasing power; the currency of Chile lost 89 per cent; of Brazil 98 per cent. The practical consequence of this is the expropriation of wealth on a tremendous scale.

Yet a United States senator, recently demanding "land reform" and ignoring this history, made it a charge against the rich in these aid-receiving nations that they do not "invest in their own economies" but place their funds abroad. What he failed to ask himself is *why* the nationals of some of these countries have been sending their funds abroad or putting them in numbered accounts in Switzerland. In most cases, he would have found that it was not only because no attractive private investment opportunities were open to them at home (because of burdensome controls, oppressive taxes, or government competition), but because they feared the wiping out of their savings by rapid depreciation of their home currencies, or even the outright confiscation of their visible wealth.

The Benefits?

In the last 23 years foreign aid has made American taxpayers $171 billion poorer, but it has not made the recipients anything like that much richer. How much good has it actually done them? The question is difficult to answer in quantitative terms, because foreign aid has often been a relatively minor factor out of the scores of factors affecting their economies.

But the advocates of foreign aid have had no trouble in giving glib and confident answers to the question.

Where, as in Western Europe and Japan, our aid has been followed by dramatic recovery, the recovery has been attributed wholly to the aid (though just as dramatic recoveries occurred in war-torn nations after World War I when there was no aid program). But where our aid has not been followed by recovery, or where recipient nations find themselves in even deeper economic crises than they were before our aid began, the aid advocates have simply said that obviously our aid was not "adequate." This argument is being used very widely today to urge us to plunge into an even more colossal aid program.

A careful country-by-country study, however, shows pretty clearly that in recent years wherever a country (such as West Germany) has reformed its currency, kept it sound, and adhered in the main to the principles of free enterprise, it has enjoyed a miraculous recovery and growth. But where a country (such as India) has chosen government planning, has adopted grandiose socialistic "five-year plans" arbitrarily directing production into the wrong lines, has expanded its currency but kept it for many years overvalued through exchange controls, and has put all sorts of restrictions and harassments in the way of private enterprise and private initiative, it has sunk into chronic crises or famine in spite of billions of dollars in generous foreign aid.

As Charles B. Shuman, president of the American Farm Bureau Federation, recently put it, the one common denominator in virtually all the hungry nations has been "their devotion to a socialist political-economic system—a government-managed economy. The world does not need to starve if the underdeveloped areas can be induced to accept a market price system, the incentive method of capital formation—competitive capitalism."

Our conclusion is that government-to-government

foreign aid, as it exists at present, is a deterrent, not a spur, to world economic prosperity, and even to the economic progress of the underdeveloped recipients themselves.

Wasteful Projects

This is true partly because of the very nature of foreign aid. By providing easy outside help without cost, it often fails to encourage self-help and responsibility. Moreover, government-to-government economic help almost inevitably goes to *government* projects, which frequently means socialized projects, such as grandiose government steel mills or power dams.

It is true that there are many economic services, such as streets and roads, water supply, harbors, and sanitary measures, that are usually undertaken by governments even in the most "capitalistic" countries, yet which form an essential basis and part of the process and structure of all production. Foreign as well as domestic funds may legitimately go to governments for such purposes. Yet intergovernmental aid is likely to channel a disproportionate amount of funds even into such projects. If governments had to depend more on domestic or foreign *private investors* for these funds, less extravagant projects of this nature would be embarked upon. Private investors, for example, might lend more freely for toll roads and bridges, and similar projects that promised to be self-liquidating, than for those that yielded no monetary return. As a result, the recipient government's planners would make more effort to put their roads and bridges where the prospective use and traffic would prove heavy enough to justify the outlay.

In addition to the conditions in the very nature of government-to-government aid that make it on net bal-

ance a deterrent rather than a spur to private enterprise
and higher production, there is the attitude of many
American aid officials, who insisted that underdeveloped nations should not get more aid unless they
adopted "land reform," planning, and other socialistic
measures—the very measures that tend to retard economic recovery.

Conditions for Private Investment

If our aid program were now tapered off, and the
underdeveloped nations had to seek foreign private
capital for their more rapid development, the case
would be far different. Foreign private investors would
want to see quite different reforms. They would want
assurance (perhaps in some cases even guarantees)
against nationalization or expropriation, against gov-
ernment-owned competition, against discriminatory
laws, against price controls, against burdensome social
security legislation, against import license difficulties
on essential materials, against currency exchange restrictions, against oppressive taxes, and against a constantly depreciating currency. They would probably
also want guarantees that they could always repatriate
their capital and profits.

Foreign private investors would not *demand* the active cooperation or an enthusiastic welcome by the government of the host country, but this would certainly
influence their decision considerably. In fact, foreign
private investors, unless the would-be borrowers came
to them, would not *demand* any conditions at all. They
would place their funds where the deterrents and dis-
couragements were fewest and the opportunities most
inviting.

What the anti-capitalistic mentality seems incapable

of understanding is that the very steps necessary to create the most attractive climate for *foreign* investment would also create the most attractive climate for *domestic* investment. The nationals of an underdeveloped country, instead of sending their money abroad for better returns or sheer safekeeping, would start investing it in enterprise at home. And this domestic investment and reinvestment would begin to make foreign investment less and less urgent.

It is unlikely that reforms in the direction of free enterprise will be made by most socialistic and control-minded countries as long as they can get intergovernmental aid without making these reforms. So a tapering off or phasing out of the American aid program will probably be necessary before a private foreign investment program is launched in sufficient volume.

A More Hopeful Alternative

I should like to renew here a suggestion for an interim program which I put forward in *National Review* of May 6, 1961: that from now on out, economic foreign aid be continued solely in the form of loans rather than grants. These would be hard loans, repayable in dollars. They would bear interest at the same rate that our own government was obliged to pay for loans of equal maturity. They would be repayable over not more than 25 to 30 years, like a mortgage. Like a mortgage, they would preferably be repayable, principal and interest, in equal monthly or quarterly installments, beginning immediately after the loan was made.

Such loans would not be urged on any country. The would-be borrowers would have to apply for them. They would be entitled to borrow annually, say, any amount up to the amount they had previously been receiving from us in grants or combined loans and grants.

All these requirements would be written into law by Congress. Congress would also write into law the conditions of eligibility for such loans. Among such conditions might be the following: The borrowing government would have to refrain from any additional socialization or nationalization of industry, or any further expropriation or seizure of capital, domestic or foreign. It would undertake to balance its budget, beginning, say, in the first full fiscal year after receiving the loan. It would undertake to halt inflation. The borrowing government, for example, might agree not to increase the quantity of money by more than 5 per cent in any one year, and not to force its central bank to buy or discount any increased amount of the government's own securities. The borrowing government might be required to dismantle any exchange controls. In brief, the borrowing country and government would be obliged to move toward the conditions that would be necessary to attract private domestic or foreign capital.

Anticipated Consequences

My guess is that the mere requirement for repayment of principal and interest, to begin immediately, would in itself probably reduce applications for aid to about a third of the amounts we now pay out. The other conditions of eligibility would probably cut the applications to a sixth or a tenth of these amounts. For the borrowing governments would have to think twice about the advisability of projects for which they would have to start paying themselves. Projects would tend to be reduced to those that were self-liquidating, i. e., demonstrably economic.

The borrowing nations could not complain that we were trying to interfere in or to dictate their domestic economic policies. These would merely be the conditions of eligibility for loans. The borrowing nations would be neither forced nor urged to borrow from us. The American administrators of the foreign loan program would not be authorized either to dictate or remove any conditions or to discriminate among borrowers. In any case, their discretion should be very narrowly circumscribed.

The benefits of such a program would be many and obvious. It would immediately cut down drastically the outflow of American funds in foreign aid. Most of the aid that we granted through such loans would be repaid with interest. We would not be courting foreign favor. The would-be borrowers would have to come to us, openly. We would cease, immediately, to subsidize and expand foreign socialism.

I should make it clear that I am not proposing such a program for its own sake, but as a purely transitional measure to phase out our existing foreign-aid program with the least possible disturbance, disruption, or recrimination. This scaled-down lending program might run for, say, a maximum of three years. At the end of that time it could easily be terminated. For meanwhile the borrowing governments, and particularly private enterprises in their respective countries, would have created an attractive climate, and would have become attractive media, for both domestic and foreign private investment.

In such a revitalized capitalistic climate, the improvement in world economic conditions might even become spectacular.

/\.\/\.\/\.\/\

CHAPTER 22

Government *Unlimited*

.\/\.\/\.\/\.\/\.\/\.\/\.\/\.\/\.\/\.\/\.\/\.\/\.\/\.\/\.\/\.\/\.\/\.\/\

SINCE THE OUTBREAK OF WORLD WAR I IN 1914, there has been an ominous growth in governmental power and intervention not only in the United States but practically all over the world. Woodrow Wilson once declared: "The history of liberty is the history of limitations of governmental power, not the increase of it." This ought to be self-evident. The greater the area of human conduct controlled by government, the smaller the area left to the individual's own control. The greater the government's power to forbid and restrict, the smaller the individual's power to choose for himself.

The growth of governmental power may be measured in terms of dollars spent, bureaucrats employed, or spheres of activity controlled.

In 1914 the Federal Government was spending only $725 million a year; in fiscal 1970 it is spending $195 *billion* a year—269 times as much.

In 1967 the number of Federal civilian employees totaled 2,877,000; the number of State and local employees 8,898,000, bringing the number employed in all government units up to 11,775,000.

In 1954 the Hoover Commission found that the Federal Government embraced no fewer than 2,133 different functioning agencies, bureaus, departments, and divisions. As Federal expenditures have more than doubled since 1954, and the number of Federal employees increased by 25 per cent, the present agency count may now exceed 2,500.

This estimate would be warranted by the known proliferation of Great Society agencies. One calculation, in 1967, counted more than 100 new Federal programs enacted by Congress since 1955; but this count was soon left far behind. In December, 1968, a departing White House aide, Joseph A. Califano, Jr., described by the New York *Times* as "President Johnson's man Friday in nurturing the Great Society," said in an interview that President-elect Richard M. Nixon would find that a tenfold growth had occurred in government activities since he left the government in January, 1961. "There were about 45 domestic social programs when the Eisenhower Administration ended," said Mr. Califano. "Now there are no less than 435."

Even this count had been exceeded earlier in 1968, when Democratic Congressman William V. Roth, Jr., and his staff were able to identify 1,571 programs, including 478 in the Department of Health, Education, and Welfare alone, but concluded that "no one, anywhere, knows exactly how many Federal programs there are." Even a prominent former interventionist confessed himself appalled by the "fantastic labyrinth of welfare programs" and the way in which the swift growth of Federal power is diminishing the significance of the individual citizen.

The growth of government power progressively breeds the growth of still more government power. The 86,000 permanent employees in the Department of Agriculture, to take but a single instance, all have a vital full-time economic interest in proving that the particular subsidies and controls they were hired to formulate and enforce should be continued and expanded. What chance does the individual disinterested citizen have— even if he has time to master the facts about the agricultural programs—in arguing against this particular bureaucratic army of 86,000?

The life of the citizen as worker, employer, enterpriser, investor, or consumer is controlled by scores of Federal agencies. Outstanding among them are the Federal Trade Commission, the Securities and Exchange Commission, the Internal Revenue Service, the Interstate Commerce Commission, the Food and Drug Administration, the Federal Communications Commission, the National Labor Relations Board. All these agencies issue rules and regulations, grant licenses, issue cease-and-desist orders, award damages, and compel individuals and corporations to do this or refrain from that. They often combine the functions of legislators, prosecutors, judges, juries, administrators. Their decisions are sometimes capricious, arbitrary, and unauthorized even by existing law. Yet when they inflict injury on corporations or individuals, or deprive them of constitutional liberties and legal rights, appeal to the courts is often difficult, costly or impossible.

The steady expansion of governmental powers also breeds nepotism and corruption in government and helps those already in power to entrench themselves— to prolong or perpetuate their hold on power. A New

York *Times* survey of patronage in the city and State
(June 17, 1968) found that "patronage has vastly expanded in the last several decades because of the tremendous growth of government, spiraling government
spending, and the expansion of government's discretionary powers to regulate, control and supervise private industry."

Yet arbitrary government power is being multiplied
daily by the now practically unchallenged assumption
that wherever there is any problem of any kind to be
solved, government is the agency to step in and solve
it. Government lawmakers or officials either already
have or demand the power to tell us just how much oil
or sugar we may import, just how many acres we may
plant to what crops, just how foodstuffs should be
packed and labelled, just how steel and copper and
drugs should be priced, just what interest rates should
be charged and how they should be calculated, just how
automobiles should be made, just what kind of artificial
eyes should be permitted, just what one group of people must do and another group must not do, just what
groups should be subsidized, and by how much, and just
which groups should be forced to subsidize them.

Should anybody be surprised that there has been an
appalling growth of crime, an outbreak of riots and a
breakdown of law enforcement? The more things a government undertakes to do, the fewer things it can do
competently. When the government tries to do everything it must do everything badly.

The essential function of the State is to maintain
peace, justice, law, and order, and to protect the individual citizen against aggression, violence, theft, and
fraud. More than a century ago Herbert Spencer was
pointing out that "in assuming any office besides its
essential one, the State begins to lose the power of
fulfilling its essential one." As more and more functions

are assumed by the State, the truth of this becomes
more and more obvious.

This brings us back once again to the warning of the
Swedish economist, Gustav Cassel, more than 30 years
ago:

> The leadership of the state in economic affairs, which ad-
> vocates of Planned Economy want to establish, is . . . neces-
> sarily connected with a bewildering mass of governmental
> interferences of a steadily cumulative nature. The arbitrari-
> ness, the mistakes, and the inevitable contradictions of such
> a policy will, as daily experience shows, only strengthen the
> demand for a more rational coordination of the different
> measures and, therefore, for unified leadership. For this rea-
> son Planned Economy will always tend to develop into Dic-
> tatorship.

In more concrete terms, the process usually runs like
this: A hundred welfare programs, spending more and
more billions, lead to chronic budget deficits, which
lead to increase paper-money issues, which lead to
higher prices. The government then denounces the
sellers as "profiteers" and starts fixing ceilings on individual prices. Next it is led inevitably into the impossible task of trying to fix all prices and wages, which
leads it to set up allocations and quotas of production
for each producer and rationing for each consumer, and
so to control of everybody's means of livelihood and
survival.

And as Alexander Hamilton once put it: "Power over
a man's subsistence is power over his will."

/\\/\.\\/\.\\/\

CHAPTER 23

From Spencer's 1884 to Orwell's 1984

\\/\.\\/\.\\/\.\\/\.\\/\.\\/\.\\/\.\\/\.\\/\.\\/\.\\/\.\\/\.\\/\.\\/\.\\/\.\\/\.\\/\

IN 1884, HERBERT SPENCER WROTE WHAT QUICKLY became a celebrated book, *The Man Versus The State.* The book is seldom referred to now, and gathers dust on library shelves—if, in fact, it is still stocked by many libraries. Spencer's political views are regarded by most present-day writers, who bother to mention him at all, as "extreme laissez faire," and hence "discredited."

But any openminded person who takes the trouble today to read or re-read *The Man Versus The State* will probably be startled by two things. The first is the uncanny clairvoyance with which Spencer foresaw what the future encroachments of the State were likely to be on individual liberty, above all in the economic realm. The second is the extent to which these encroachments

had already occurred in 1884, the year in which he was
writing.

The present generation has been brought up to believe that government concern for "social justice" and
for the plight of the needy was something that did not
even exist until the New Deal came along in 1933. The
ages prior to that have been pictured as periods when
no one "cared," when laissez faire was rampant, when
everybody who did not succeed in the cutthroat competition that was euphemistically called free enterprise
—but was simply a system of dog-eat-dog and the-devil-
take-the-hindmost—was allowed to starve. And if the
present generation thinks this is true even of the Nineteen Twenties, it is absolutely convinced that this was
so in the Eighteen Eighties, which it would probably
regard as the very peak of the prevalence of laissez
faire.

Yet the new reader's initial astonishment when he
starts Spencer's book may begin to wear off before he
is halfway through, because one cause for surprise ex-
plains the other. All that Spencer was doing was to
project or extrapolate the legislative tendencies existing in the Eighteen Eighties into the future. It was
because he was so clearsightedly appalled by these tendencies that he recognized them so much more sharply
than his contemporaries, and saw so much more clearly
where they would lead if left unchecked.

Even in his Preface to *The Man Versus The State* he
pointed out how "increase of freedom in form" was
being followed by "decrease of freedom in fact. . . .

Regulations have been made in yearly growing numbers,
restraining the citizen in directions where his actions were
previously unchecked, and compelling actions which previously he might perform or not as he liked; and at the same
time heavier public burdens . . . have further restricted his

freedom, by lessening that portion of his earnings which he can spend as he pleases, and augmenting the portion taken from him to be spent as public agents please.

In his first chapter, "The New Toryism," Spencer contends that "most of those who now pass as Liberals, are Tories of a new type." The Liberals of his own day, he points out, had already "lost sight of the truth that in past times Liberalism habitually stood for individual freedom versus State-coercion."

So the complete Anglo-American switch of reference, by which a "liberal" today has come to mean primarily a State interventionist, had already begun in 1884. Already "plausible proposals" were being made "that there should be organized a system of compulsory insurance, by which men during their early lives shall be forced to provide for the time when they will be incapacitated." Here is already the seed of the American Social Security Act of 1935.

Spencer also pays his respects to the anti-libertarian implications of an increasing tax burden. Those who impose additional taxes are saying in effect: "Hitherto you have been free to spend this portion of your earnings in any way which pleased you; hereafter you shall not be free to spend it, but we will spend it for the general benefit."

Spencer next turns to the compulsions that unions were even then imposing on their members, and asks: "If men use their liberty in such a way as to surrender their liberty, are they thereafter any the less slaves?"

In his second chapter, "The Coming Slavery," Spencer calls attention to the existence of what he calls "political momentum"—the tendency of State interventions and similar political measures to increase and accelerate in the direction in which they have already

been set going. Americans have become only too familiar with this momentum in the last few years.

Spencer illustrates: "The blank form of an inquiry
daily made is—'We have already done this; why should
we not do that?'" "The buying and working of tele-
graphs by the State" (which already operated them in
England when he wrote), he continued, "is made a
reason for urging that the State should buy and work
the railways." And he went on to quote the demands of
one group that the State should take possession of the
railways, "with or without compensation."

The British State did not buy and work the railways
until 65 years later, in 1948, but it did get around to it,
precisely as Spencer feared.

It is not only precedent that prompts the constant
spread of interventionist measures, Spencer points out,

but also the necessity which arises for supplementing ineffective measures, and for dealing with the artificial evils
continually caused. Failure does not destroy faith in the agencies employed, but merely suggests more stringent use of
such agencies or wider ramifications of them.

One illustration he gives is how "the evils produced
by compulsory charity are now proposed to be met by
compulsory insurance." Today, in America, one could
point to scores of examples (from measures to cure "the
deficit in the balance of payments" to the constant multiplication of measures to fight the government's "war
on poverty") of interventions mainly designed to
remove the artificial evils brought about by previous
interventions.

Everywhere, Spencer goes on, the tacit assumption is
that "government should step in whenever anything is
not going right. . . . The more numerous governmental
interventions become . . . the more loud and perpetual

the demands for interventions." Every additional relief measure raises hopes of further ones:

> The more numerous public instrumentalities become, the more is there generated in citizens the notion that everything is to be done for them, and nothing by them. Every generation is made less familiar with the attainment of desired ends by individual actions or private agencies; until, eventually, governmental agencies come to be thought of as the only available agencies.

"All socialism," Spencer concludes, "involves slavery. . . . That which fundamentally distinguishes the slave is that he labors under coercion to satisfy another's desires." The relation admits of many gradations. Oppressive taxation is a form of slavery of the individual to the community as a whole. "The essential question is—How much is he compelled to labor for other benefit than his own, and how much can he labor for his own benefit?"

Even Spencer would probably have regarded with incredulity a prediction that in less than two generations England would have rates of income tax rising above 90 per cent, and that many an energetic and ambitious man, in England and the United States, would be forced to spend more than half his time and labor working for the support of the community, and allowed less than half his time and labor to provide for his own family and himself.

Today's progressive income tax provides a quantitative measurement of the relative extent of a man's economic liberty and servitude.

Those who think that public housing is an entirely new development will be startled to hear that the beginnings of it—as well as some of its harmful consequences—were already present in 1884:

Where municipal bodies turn house-builders [wrote Spencer], they inevitably lower the values of houses otherwise built, and check the supply of more. . . . The multiplication of houses, and especially small houses, being increasingly checked, there must come an increasing demand upon the local authority to make up for the deficient supply. . . . And then when in towns this process has gone so far as to make the local authority the chief owner of houses, there will be a good precedent for publicly providing houses for the rural population, as proposed in the Radical program, and as urged by the Democratic Federation [which insists on] the compulsory construction of healthy artisans' and agricultural laborers' dwellings in proportion to the population.

One State intervention Spencer did not foresee was the future imposition of rent controls, which make it unprofitable for private persons to own, repair, or renovate old rental housing or to put up new. The consequences of rent control provoke the indignant charge that "private enterprise is simply not doing the job" of providing enough housing. The conclusion is that therefore the government must step in and take over that job.

What Spencer did expressly fear, in another field, was that public education, providing gratis what private schools had to charge for, would in time destroy the private schools. But of course he did not foresee that eventually the government would provide free tuition even in tax-supported *colleges* and universities, thus more and more threatening the continuance of private colleges and universities—and so tending more and more to produce a uniform conformist education, with college faculties ultimately dependent for their jobs on the government, and so developing an economic interest in professing and teaching a statist, pro-government, and socialist ideology. The tendency of government-supported education must be finally to achieve a government monopoly of education.

As the "liberal" readers of 1970 may be shocked to learn that the recent State interventions that they regard as the latest expressions of advanced and compassionate thought were anticipated in 1884, so the statist readers of Spencer's day must have been shocked to learn from him how many of the latest State interventions of 1884 were anticipated in Roman times and in the Middle Ages. For Spencer reminded them, quoting an historian, that in Gaul, during the decline of the Roman Empire, "so numerous were the receivers in comparison with the payers, and so enormous the weight of taxation, that the laborer broke down, the plains became deserts, and woods grew where the plough had been."

Spencer reminded his readers also of the usury laws under Louis XV in France, which raised the rate of interest "from five to six when intending to reduce it to four." He reminded them of the laws against "forestalling" (buying up goods in advance for later resale), also in early France. The effect of such laws was to prevent anyone from buying "more than two bushels of wheat at market," which prevented traders and dealers from equalizing supplies over time, thereby intensifying scarcities. He reminded his readers also of the measure which, in 1315, to diminish the pressure of famine, prescribed the prices of foods, but which was later repealed after it had caused the entire disappearance of various foods from the markets. He reminded them, again, of the many endeavors to fix wages, beginning with the Statute of Laborers under Edward III (1327-77). And still again, of Statute 35 of Edward III, which aimed to keep down the price of herring (but was soon repealed because it raised the price). And yet again, of the law of Edward III, under which innkeepers at seaports were sworn to search their guests "to prevent the exportation of money or plate."

This last example will remind Americans uneasily of the present prohibition of private gold holdings and gold export, and of the Johnson Administration's proposal to put a punitive tax on foreign travel, as well as the actual punitive tax that it did put on foreign investment. Let us add the still existing prohibitions even by allegedly advanced European nations against taking more than a tiny amount of their local *paper* currency out of the country!

I come to one last specific parallel between 1884 and the present. This concerns slum clearance and urban renewal. The British government of Spencer's day responded to the existence of wretched and over crowded housing by enacting the Artisans' Dwellings Acts. These gave to local authorities powers to pull down bad houses and provide for the building of good ones:

What have been the results? A summary of the operations of the Metropolitan Board of Works, dated December 21, 1883, shows that up to last September it had, at a cost of a million and a quarter to ratepayers, unhoused 21,000 persons and provided houses for 12,000—the remaining 9,000 to be hereafter provided for, being, meanwhile, left houseless. This is not all. . . . Those displaced . . . form a total of nearly 11,000 artificially made homeless, who have had to find corners for themselves in miserable places that were already overflowing.

Those who are interested in a thorough study of the present-day parallel to this are referred to Professor Martin Anderson's *The Federal Bulldozer* (M. I. T. Press, 1964; McGraw-Hill paperback, 1967). I quote just one short paragraph from his findings:

The Federal urban renewal program has actually aggravated the housing shortage for low-income groups. From 1950 to 1960, 126,000 dwelling units, most of them low-rent ones, were destroyed. This study estimates that the number of new dwelling units constructed is less than one-fourth of the number demolished, and that most of the new units are high-rent ones. Contrast the net addition of millions of standard dwelling units to the housing supply by private enterprise with the minute construction effort of the Federal urban renewal program. [P. 229]

There is an eloquent paragraph in Spencer's book reminding his readers of the Eighties of what they did *not* owe to the State:

It is not to the State that we owe the multitudinous useful inventions from the spade to the telephone; it is not the State which made possible extended navigation by a developed astronomy; it was not the State which made the discoveries in physics, chemistry, and the rest, which guide modern manufacturers; it was not the State which devised the machinery for producing fabrics of every kind, for transferring men and things from place to place, and for ministering in a thousand ways to our comforts. The world-wide transactions conducted in merchants' offices, the rush of traffic filling our streets, the retail distributing system which brings everything within easy reach and delivers the necessaries of life daily at our doors, are not of governmental origin. All these are results of the spontaneous activities of citizens, separate or grouped.

Our present-day statists are busily trying to change all this. They are seizing billions of additional dollars from the taxpayers to turn them over for "scientific research." By this compulsorily subsidized government competition they are discouraging and draining away the funds for private scientific research; and they threaten to make research, in time, a government monopoly. But whether this will result in more scientific progress in the long run is doubtful. True, enormously more money is being spent on "research," but it is being diverted in questionable directions—in military research; in developing greater and greater super-bombs and other weapons of mass destruction and mass annihilation; in planning supersonic passenger airplanes developed on the assumption that civilians must get to their European or Caribbean vacation spots at 1,200 or 1,800 miles an hour, instead of a mere 600, no matter how many eardrums or windows of groundlings are shattered in the process; and finally, in such Buck Rogers stunts as landing men on the moon (however breathtaking that achievement) or even on Mars. It is not what scientists think is most important or urgent, but what politicians decide will most impress and astound the masses, that determines the direction of research.

It is fairly obvious that all this will involve enormous waste; that government bureaucrats will be able to dictate who gets the research funds and who doesn't, and that this choice will depend either upon fixed arbitrary qualifications like those determined by Civil Service examinations (hardly the way to find the most original minds), or upon the grantees keeping in the good graces of the particular government appointee in charge of the distribution of grants.

But our welfare statists seem determined to put us in a position where we will be dependent on government even for our future scientific and industrial progress— or in a position where they can at least plausibly argue that we are so dependent.

Spencer next goes on to show that the kind of State intervention he is deploring amounts not merely to an abridgment but a basic rejection of private property: a "confusion of ideas, caused by looking at one face only of the transaction, may be traced throughout all the legislation which forcibly takes the property of this man for the purpose of giving gratis benefits to that man." The tacit assumption underlying all these acts of redistribution is that:

No man has any claim to his property, not even to that which he has earned by the sweat of his brow, save by the permission of the community; and that the community may cancel the claim to any extent it thinks fit. No defense can be made for this appropriation of A's possessions for the benefit of B, save one which sets out with the postulate that society as a whole has an absolute right over the possessions of each member.

In the final chapter (just preceding a Postscript) Spencer concluded: "The function of Liberalism in the past was that of putting a limit to the powers of kings. The function of true Liberalism in the future will be that of putting a limit to the power of Parliaments."

In endorsing some of the arguments in Spencer's *The Man Versus the State,* and in recognizing the penetration of many of his insights and the remarkable accuracy of his predictions of the political future, we need not necessarily subscribe to every position that he took. The very title of Spencer's book was in one respect unfortunate. To speak of "the man versus the state" is to imply that the State, *as such,* is unnecessary and evil. The State, of course, is absolutely indispensable to the preservation of law and order, and the promotion of peace and social cooperation. What is unnecessary and evil, what abridges the liberty and threatens the true welfare of the individual, is the State that has usurped excessive powers and grown beyond its legitimate functions—the super-State, the socialist State, the redistributive State, in brief, the ironically misnamed "Welfare State."

Again, we need not accept Spencer's own "first principle" (as laid down in his *Social Statics* in 1850) for determining the function of law and the limits of the State: "Every man has freedom to do all he wills, provided he infringes not the equal freedom of any other man." Taken literally, this could be interpreted to mean that a thug has the right to stand at a corner with a club and beat over the head everybody who comes round it, provided he acknowledges the right of any of his victims to do the same.

At least, Spencer's principle seems to permit any amount of mutual annoyance except constraint. It is entirely true, as Locke pointed out, that "the end of the law is, not to abolish or restrain, but to preserve and enlarge freedom." But the only short formula we can use to describe the function of the law would be that it should maximize liberty, order, and happiness by minimizing constraint, violence, and harm. The detailed application of any such simple formula presents many difficulties and problems. We need not go into them here, except to say that the Common Law, developed from ancient custom and a hundred thousand decisions of judges, has been solving these problems through the ages, and that in our age jurists and economists have been further refining these decisions.

But Spencer was certainly right in the main thrust of his argument, which was essentially that of Adam Smith and other classical liberals, that the two indispensable functions of government are first, to protect the nation against aggression from any other nation, and second, to protect the individual citizen from the aggression, injustice, or oppression of any other citizen—and that every extension of the functions of government beyond these two primary duties should be scrutinized with jealous vigilance.

Another issue on which we need not necessarily

agree with Spencer was his complete rejection of State
relief, based on an inflexible and doctrinaire application of his doctrine of "survival of the fittest." He was
quite right in quoting approvingly from a report of the
old Poor Law Commissioners: "We find, on the one
hand, that there is scarcely one statute connected with
the administration of public relief which has produced
the effect designed by the legislature, and that the
majority of them have created new evils, and aggravated those which they were intended to prevent."
This judgment could be obviously applied with even
greater force to the enormous proliferation, expansion,
and amendments of relief measures today.

Yet though the problem of the relief of poverty and
misfortune has not been solved, we cannot callously
deny that the problem exists. Nor can we leave its solution entirely to private charity. To cite an extreme example, but unfortunately one of daily occurrence: If a
child is run over in the street or if two cars crash, there
ought to be the quickest possible provision for taking
and admitting the victim or victims immediately to a
hospital, if necessary, before there has been time to
determine whether or not they can afford to pay for
doctor or hospital service, and without depending on
the offer of some private good Samaritan, who may or
may not happen to be on the scene, to guarantee payment of the hospital bill. There should be governmental
provision to meet all such emergencies.

The great problem is, of course, how to provide such
emergency relief without allowing it to degenerate into
permanent relief; how to relieve the extreme distress of
those who are poor through little or no fault of their
own, without supporting in idleness those who are poor
mainly or entirely through fault of their own. To state
the problem in another way (as I have earlier done):
How can we mitigate the penalties of failure and mis-

fortune without undermining the incentives to effort and success? In what precise cases and to what precise extent is it the State's duty to play a role in the solution of this problem? And what exactly should that role be? Over three thousand years of history this problem has never been satisfactorily solved by any government anywhere. I do not pretend to know the precise solution. But the two-sidedness of the problem of relieving suffering without destroying incentive must be frankly recognized by both "conservatives" and "liberals," and there is at least a gain in stating it candidly and clearly.

Yet whatever reservations or qualifications we may have, we are deeply indebted to Herbert Spencer for recognizing with a sharper eye than any of his contemporaries, and warning them against, "the coming slavery" toward which the State of their own time was drifting, and toward which we are more swiftly drifting today.

It is more than a grim coincidence that Spencer was warning of the coming slavery in 1884, and that George Orwell, in our time, has predicted that the full consummation of this slavery will be reached in 1984, exactly one century later.

/.\/.\/.\/.\

CHAPTER 24

The Task Confronting Libertarians

/.\

FROM TIME TO TIME OVER THE LAST THIRTY YEARS, after I have talked or written about some new restriction on human liberty in the economic field, some new attack on private enterprise, I have been asked in person or received a letter asking, "What can *I* do"—to fight the inflationist or socialist trend? Other writers or lecturers, I find, are often asked the same question.

The answer is seldom an easy one. For it depends on the circumstances and ability of the questioner—who may be a businessman, a housewife, a student, informed or not, intelligent or not, articulate or not. And the answer must vary with these presumed circumstances.

The general answer is easier than the particular an-

swer. So here I want to write about the task now confronting all libertarians considered collectively.

This task has become tremendous, and seems to grow
greater every day. A few nations that have already gone
completely Communist, like Soviet Russia and its satel-
lites, try, as a result of sad experience, to draw back a
little from complete centralization, and experiment
with one or two quasi-capitalist techniques; but the
world's prevailing drift—in more than 100 out of the 111
or so nations and mini-nations that are now members of
the International Monetary Fund—is in the direction of
increasing socialism and controls.

The task of the tiny minority that is trying to combat
this socialistic drift seems nearly hopeless. The war
must be fought on a thousand fronts, and the true libertarians are grossly outnumbered on practically all these
fronts.

In a thousand fields the welfarists, statists, socialists,
and interventionists are daily driving for more restrictions on individual liberty; and the libertarians must
combat them. But few of us individually have the time,
energy, and special knowledge in more than a handful
of subjects to be able to do this.

One of our gravest problems is that we find ourselves
confronting the armies of bureaucrats who already control us, and who have a vested interest in keeping and
expanding the controls they were hired to enforce.

A Growing Bureaucracy

I pointed out in Chapter 22 that the Federal Government now embraces some 2,500 different functioning
agencies, bureaus, departments, and divisions. Federal
full-time permanent civilian employees are estimated
to reach 2,693,508 as of June 30, 1970.

And we know, to take a few specific examples, that of these bureaucrats 16,800 administer the programs of the Department of Housing and Urban Development, 106,700 the programs (including Social Security) of the Department of Health, Education, and Welfare, and 152,300 the programs of the Veterans Administration.

If we want to look at the rate at which parts of this bureaucracy have been growing, let us refer again to the Department of Agriculture. In 1929, before the United States Government started crop controls and price supports on an extensive scale, there were 24,000 employees in that Department. Today, counting part-time workers, there are 120,000, five times as many, all of them with a vital economic interest—to wit, their own jobs—in proving that the particular controls they were hired to formulate and enforce should be continued and expanded.

What chance does the individual businessman, the occasional disinterested professor of economics, or columnist, or editorial writer, have in arguing against the policies and actions of this 120,000-man army, even if he has had time to learn the detailed facts of a particular issue? His criticisms are either ignored or drowned out in the organized counterstatements.

This is only one example out of scores. A few of us may suspect that there is much unjustified or foolish expenditure in the United States Social Security program, or that the unfunded liabilities already undertaken by the program (one authoritative estimate of these exceeds a *trillion* dollars) may prove to be unpayable without a gross monetary inflation. A handful of us may suspect that the whole principle of compulsory government old age and survivor's insurance is open to question. But there are some 100,000 full-time permanent employees in the Department of Health, Education, and Welfare to dismiss all such fears as foolish, and to insist that we are still not doing nearly enough for our older citizens, our sick, and our widows and orphans.

And then there are the millions of those who are already on the receiving end of these payments, who have come to consider them as an earned right, who of course find them inadequate, and who are outraged at the slightest suggestion of a critical re-examination of the subject. The political pressure for constant extension and increase of these benefits is almost irresistible.

And even if there weren't whole armies of government economists, statisticians, and administrators to answer him, the lone disinterested critic, who hopes to have his criticism heard and respected by other disinterested and thoughtful people, finds himself compelled to keep up with appalling mountains of detail.

Too Many Cases to Follow

The National Labor Relations Board, for example, hands down hundreds of decisions every year in passing on "unfair" labor practices. In the fiscal year 1967 it passed on 803 cases "contested as to the law and the facts." Most of these decisions are strongly biased in favor of the labor unions; many of them pervert the intention of the Taft-Hartley Act that they ostensibly enforce; and in some of them the Board arrogates to itself powers that go far beyond those granted by the Act. The texts of many of these decisions are very long in their statement of facts or alleged facts and of the Board's conclusions. How is the individual economist or editor to keep abreast of the decisions and to comment informedly and intelligently on those that involve an important principle or public interest?

Or take again such major agencies as the Federal Trade Commission, the Securities and Exchange Commission, the Food and Drug Administration, the Federal Communications Commission. These agencies, as I pointed out in Chapter 22, often combine the functions of legislators, prosecutors, judges, juries, and administrators.

Yet how can the individual economist, student of government, journalist, or anyone interested in defending or preserving liberty, hope to keep abreast of this Niagara of decisions, regulations, and administrative laws? He may sometimes consider himself lucky to be able to master in many months the facts concerning one of these decisions.

Professor Sylvester Petro of New York University has written a full book on the Kohler strike and another full book on the Kingsport strike, and the public lessons to be learned from them. Professor Martin Anderson has specialized in the follies of urban renewal programs. But how many are there among those of us who call ourselves libertarians who are willing—or have the time —to do this specialized and microscopic but indispensable research?

In July, 1967, the Federal Communications Commission handed down an extremely harmful decision ordering the American Telephone and Telegraph Company to lower its interstate rates—which were already 20 per cent lower than in 1940, though the general price level since that time had gone up 163 per cent. In order to write a single editorial or column on this (and to feel confident he had his facts straight), a conscientious journalist had to study, among other material, the text of the decision. That decision consisted of 114 single-spaced typewritten pages.

. . . and Schemes for Reform

We libertarians have our work cut out for us.

In order to indicate further the dimensions of this work, it is not merely the organized bureaucracy that the libertarian has to answer; it is the individual private zealots. A day never passes without some ardent reformer or group of reformers suggesting some new government intervention, some new statist scheme to fill some alleged "need" or relieve some alleged distress. They accompany their scheme by elaborate statistics that supposedly prove the need or the distress that they want the taxpayers to relieve. So it comes about that the reputed "experts" on relief, unemployment insurance, Social Security, Medicare, subsidized housing, foreign aid, and the like are precisely the people who are advocating more relief, unemployment insurance, Social Security, Medicare, subsidized housing, foreign aid, and all the rest.

Let us come to some of the lessons we must draw from all this.

Specialists for the Defense

We libertarians cannot content ourselves merely with repeating pious generalities about liberty, free enterprise, and limited government. To assert and repeat these general principles is absolutely necessary, of course, either as prologue or conclusion. But if we hope to be individually or collectively effective, we must individually master a great deal of detailed knowledge, and make ourselves specialists in one or two lines, so that we can show how our libertarian principles apply in special fields, and so that we can convincingly dispute the proponents of statist schemes for public housing, farm subsidies, increased relief, bigger Social Security benefits, bigger Medicare, guaranteed incomes, bigger government spending, bigger taxation, especially more progressive income taxation, higher tariffs or import quotas, restrictions or penalties on foreign investment and foreign travel, price controls, wage controls, rent controls, interest rate controls, more laws for so-called "consumer protection," and still tighter regulations and restrictions on business everywhere.

This means, among other things, that libertarians must form and maintain organizations not only to promote their broad principles—as do, for example, the Foundation for Economic Education at Irvington-on-Hudson, N. Y., the American Institute for Economic Research at Great Barrington, Mass., and the American Economic Foundation in New York City—but to promote these principles in special fields. I am thinking, for example, of such excellent existing specialized organizations as the Citizens Foreign Aid Committee, the Economists' National Committee on Monetary Policy, the Tax Foundation, and so on.

We need not fear that too many of these specialized organizations will be formed. The real danger is the opposite. The private libertarian organizations in the United States are probably outnumbered ten to one by Communist, socialist, statist, and other left-wing organizations that have shown themselves to be only too effective.

And I am sorry to report that almost none of the old-line business associations that I am acquainted with are as effective as they could be. It is not merely that they have been timorous or silent where they should have spoken out, or even that they have unwisely compromised. Recently, for fear of being called ultraconservative or reactionary, they have been supporting measures harmful to the very interests they were formed to protect. Several of them, for example, came out in favor of the Johnson Administration's tax increase on corporations in 1968, because they were afraid to say that that Administration ought rather to have slashed its profligate welfare spending.

The sad fact is that today most of the heads of big businesses in America have become so confused or intimidated that, so far from carrying the argument to the enemy, they fail to defend themselves adequately even when attacked. The pharmaceutical industry, subjected since 1962 to a discriminatory law that applies questionable and dangerous legal principles which the government has not yet dared to apply in other fields, has been too timid to present its own case effectively. And the automobile makers, attacked by a single zealot for turning out cars "unsafe at any speed," handled the matter with an incredible combination of neglect and ineptitude that brought down on their heads legislation harmful not only to the industry but to the driving public.

The Timidity of Businessmen

It is impossible to tell today where the anti-business sentiment in Washington, plus the itch for more government control, is going to strike next. In 1967 Congress allowed itself to be stampeded into a dubious extension of Federal power over intrastate meat sales. In 1968 it passed a "truth-in-lending" law, forcing lenders to calculate and state interest rates the way Federal bureaucrats want them calculated and stated. When, in January, 1968, President Johnson suddenly announced that he was prohibiting American business from making further direct investments in Europe, and that he was restricting them elsewhere, most newspapers and businessmen, instead of raising a storm of protest against these unprecedented invasions of our liberties, deplored their "necessity" and hoped they would be only "temporary."

The very existence of the business timidity that allows these things to happen is evidence that government controls and power are already excessive.

Why are the heads of big business in America so timid? That is a long story, but I will suggest a few reasons: (1) They may be entirely or largely dependent on government war contracts. (2) They never know when or on what grounds they will be held guilty of violating the antitrust laws. (3) They never know when or on what grounds the National Labor Relations Board will hold them guilty of unfair labor practices. (4) They never know when their personal income tax returns will be hostilely examined, and they are certainly not confident that such an examination, and its findings, will be entirely independent of whether they have been personally friendly or hostile to the Administration in power.

It will be noticed that the governmental actions or laws of which businessmen stand in fear are actions or laws that leave a great deal to administrative discretion. Discretionary administrative law should be reduced to a minimum; it breeds bribery and corruption, and is always potentially blackmail or blackjack law.

Schumpeter's Indictment

Libertarians are learning to their sorrow that big businessmen cannot necessarily be relied upon to be their allies in the battle against extension of governmental encroachments. The reasons are many. Sometimes businessmen will advocate tariffs, import quotas, subsidies, and restrictions of competition, because they think, rightly or wrongly, that these government interventions will be in their personal interest, or in the interest of their companies, and are not concerned whether or not they may be at the expense of the general public. More often, I think, businessmen advocate these interventions because they are honestly confused, because they just don't realize what the actual consequences will be of the particular measures they propose, or fail to perceive the cumulative debilitating effects of growing restrictions on human liberty.

Perhaps most often of all, however, businessmen today acquiesce in new government controls out of sheer timidity.

A generation ago, in his pessimistic book, *Capitalism, Socialism and Democracy* (1942), the late Joseph A. Schumpeter maintained the thesis that "in the capitalistic system there is a tendency toward self-destruction." And as one evidence of this he cited the "cowardice" of big businessmen when facing direct attack:

They talk and plead—or hire people to do it for them; they snatch at every chance of compromise; they are ever ready to give in; they never put up a fight under the flag of their own ideals and interests—in this country there was no real resistance anywhere against the imposition of crushing financial burdens during the last decade or against labor legislation incompatible with the effective management of industry.

So much for the formidable problems facing dedicated libertarians. They find it extremely difficult to defend particular firms and industries from harassment or persecution when those industries will not adequately or competently defend themselves. Yet division of labor is both possible and desirable in the defense of liberty, as it is in other fields. And many, who have neither the time nor the specialized knowledge to analyze particular industries or special complex problems, can be nonetheless effective in the libertarian cause by hammering incessantly on some single principle or point until it is driven home.

Some Basic Principles

Is there any single principle or point on which libertarians could most effectively concentrate? Let us look, and we may end by finding not one but several.

One simple truth that could be endlessly reiterated, and effectively applied to nine-tenths of the statist proposals now being put forward or enacted in such profusion, is that the government has nothing to give to anybody that it doesn't first take from somebody else. In other words, all its relief and subsidy schemes are merely ways of robbing Peter to support Paul.

Thus, it can be pointed out (as we did in Chapter 16) that the modern Welfare State is merely a complicated arrangement by which nobody pays for the education of his own children, but everybody pays for the education of everybody else's children; by which nobody pays his own medical bills, but everybody pays everybody else's medical bills; by which nobody provides for his own old-age security, but everybody pays for everybody else's old-age security; and so on. As noted before, Bastiat exposed the illusive character of all these welfare schemes more than a century ago in his aphorism: "The State is the great fiction by which everybody tries to live at the expense of everybody else."

Another way of showing what is wrong with all the State handout schemes is to keep pointing out that you can't get a quart out of a pint jug. Or, as the State giveaway programs must all be paid for out of taxation, with each new scheme proposed the libertarian can ask, *"Instead of what?"* Thus, if it is proposed to spend another $1 billion on putting more men on the moon or developing a supersonic commercial plane, it may be pointed out that this $1 billon, taken in taxation, will not then be able to meet a million personal needs or wants of the millions of taxpayers from whom it is to be taken.

Of course, some champions of ever-greater governmental power and spending recognize this very well, and like Professor J. K. Galbraith, for instance, they invent the theory that the taxpayers, left to themselves, spend the money they have earned very foolishly, on all sorts of trivialities and rubbish, and that only the bureaucrats, by first seizing it from them, will know how to spend it wisely.

Knowing the Consequences

Another very important principle to which the libertarian can constantly appeal is to ask the statists to consider the secondary and long-run consequences of their proposals as well as merely their intended direct and immediate consequences. The statists will sometimes admit quite freely, for example, that they have nothing to give to anybody that they must not first take from somebody else. They will admit that they must rob Peter to pay Paul. But their argument is that they are seizing only from rich Peter to support poor Paul. As President Johnson once put it quite frankly in a speech on January 15, 1964: "We are going to try to take all of the money that we think is unnecessarily being spent and take it from the 'haves' and give it to the 'have nots' that need it so much."

Those who have the habit of considering long-run consequences will recognize that all these programs for sharing the wealth and guaranteeing incomes must reduce incentives at both ends of the economic scale. They must reduce the incentives both of those who are capable of earning a higher income, but find it taken away from them, and those who are capable of earning at least a moderate income, but find themselves supplied with the necessities of life without working.

This vital consideration of incentives is almost systematically overlooked in the proposals of agitators for more and bigger government welfare schemes. We should all be concerned about the plight of the poor and unfortunate. But the hard two-part question that any plan for relieving poverty must answer is: How can we mitigate the penalties of failure and misfortune *without undermining the incentives to effort and success?* Most of our would-be reformers and humanitarians simply ignore the second half of this problem. And when those of us who advocate freedom of enterprise are compelled to reject one of these specious "antipoverty" schemes after another on the ground that it will undermine these incentives and in the long run produce more evil than good, we are accused by the demagogues and the thoughtless of being "negative" and stony-hearted obstructionists. But the libertarian must have the strength not to be intimidated by this.

Finally, the libertarian who wishes to hammer in a few general principles can repeatedly appeal to the enormous advantages of liberty as compared with coercion. But he, too, will have influence and perform his duty properly only if he has arrived at his principles through careful study and thought. "The common people of England," once wrote Adam Smith, "are very jealous of their liberty, but like the common people of most other countries have never rightly understood in what it consists." To arrive at the proper concept and definition of liberty is difficult, not easy.*

Legal and Political Aspects

So far, I have written as if the libertarian's study, thought, and argument need be confined solely to the field of economics. But, of course, liberty cannot be enlarged or preserved unless its necessity is understood in many other fields—and most notably in law and in politics.

We have to ask, for example, whether liberty, economic progress, and political stability can be preserved if we continue to allow the people on relief—the people who are mainly or solely supported by the government and who live at the expense of the taxpayers—to exercise the franchise. I have already pointed out, in Chapter 11, that the great liberals of the nineteenth and early twentieth centuries, including John Stuart Mill and A. V. Dicey, expressed the most serious misgivings on this point.

An Honest Currency and an End to Inflation

This brings me, finally, to one more single issue on which all those libertarians who lack the time or background for specialized study can effectively concentrate. This is in demanding that the government provide an honest currency, and that it stop inflating.

This issue has the inherent advantage that it can be made clear and simple because fundamentally it *is* clear and simple. All inflation is government-made. All inflation is the result of increasing the quantity of money and credit; and the cure is simply to halt the increase.

*I strongly recommend *The Constitution of Liberty,* by F. A. Hayek (University of Chicago Press, 1960).

If libertarians lose on the inflation issue, they are threatened with the loss of every other issue. If libertarians could win the inflation issue, they could come close to winning everything else. If they could succeed in halting the increase in the quantity of money, it would be because they could halt the chronic deficits that force this increase. If they could halt these chronic deficits, it would be because they had halted the rapid increase in welfare spending and all the socialistic schemes that are dependent on welfare spending. If they could halt the constant increase in spending, they could halt the constant increase in government power.

The devaluation of the British pound, first in 1949 and again in 1967, may as an offset have the longer effect of helping the libertarian cause. It exposes the bankruptcy of the Welfare State. It exposes the fragility and complete undependability of the paper-gold international monetary system under which the world has been operating since 1944. There is hardly one of the hundred or more currencies in the International Monetary Fund, with the exception of the dollar, that has not been devalued at least once since the IMF opened its doors for business. There is not a single currency unit—and there is no exception to this statement—that does not buy less today than when the Fund started.

At the moment of writing this, the dollar, to which practically every other currency is tied in the present system, is in the gravest peril. If liberty is to be preserved, the world must eventually get back to a full gold standard system in which each major country's currency unit must be convertible into gold on demand, by anybody who holds it, without discrimination. I am aware that some technical defects can be pointed out in the gold standard, but it has one virtue that more than outweighs them all. It is not, like paper money, subject to the day-to-day whims of the politicians; it cannot be printed or otherwise manipulated by the politicians; it frees the individual holder from that form of swindling or expropriation by the politicians; it is an essential safeguard for the preservation, not only of the value of the currency unit itself, but of human liberty. Every libertarian should support it.

I have one last word. In whatever field he specializes, or on whatever principle or issue he elects to take his stand, the libertarian *must* take a stand. He cannot afford to do or say nothing. I have only to remind him of the eloquent call to battle on the final page of Ludwig von Mises's great book, *Socialism*, written 35 years ago:

Everyone carries a part of society on his shoulders; no one is relieved of his share of responsibility by others. And no one can find a safe way out for himself if society is sweeping toward destruction. Therefore everyone, in his own interests, must thrust himself vigorously into the intellectual battle. None can stand aside with unconcern; the interests of everyone hang on the result. Whether he chooses or not, every man is drawn into the great historical struggle, the decisive battle into which our epoch has plunged us.

/\\\/\\\/\\\/\\\/\\\/\\\

CHAPTER 25

What We Can Do About It

/\\

IF THE WELFARIST-SOCIALIST-INFLATIONIST TREND
of recent years continues in this country, the outlook is
dark. It is a prospect of mounting taxation, snowballing
expenditures, chronic deficits, a budget out of control,
an accelerating rate of inflation of the kind endemic in
Latin America (at least for the last generation), a collapse of the dollar, increasing world currency chaos,
and more and more ruthless price, wage, and exchange
controls, leading toward a regimented economy and
dictatorship. And if this trend is interrupted temporarily, it may be by riots, assassinations, and a breakdown of law and order.

But it is within our power not only to avert this night-
marish prospect, but to restore order, justice, constitu-

tionalism, limited government, economic and personal liberty, internal peace, and stable prosperity and growth.

The remedies we must apply are implicit in the evils already described. We must halt and in most cases reverse the "remedies" that have brought us to our present predicament. In the last chapter we discussed at length, but also in a rather random way, a few of the true remedies which libertarians should support. But by way of summing up, I should like to list here, even at the cost of some repetition and overlap, just eight real cures of our present political and economic disorders based on the analysis in the preceding chapters.

1. We must start reducing the grossly extended powers of all levels of government, local, State, and Federal. We must start decentralizing power, not only from the Federal Government back to the States and localities, but *within* each level of government, especially the Federal. The powers of the American presidency have grown beyond the ability of any human being to exercise them responsibly and wisely.

The crying need today is not for more laws, but for fewer. The world must be saved from its saviors. If the friends of liberty and law could have only one slogan it should be: Stop the remedies! *Stop the remedies!* Or even shorter: Repeal! *Repeal!*

2. Stop the profligate spending. Stop the deficits. Return to balanced budgets as the norm rather than the exception. Stop the constant increase in the national debt. Stop the inflation.

3. To stop the inflation, the government must stop expanding the issue of paper money and credit.

The International Monetary Fund ought to be dismantled. The Articles of Agreement should at least be amended to remove all provisions that oblige the strong currencies to support the weak—in other words, that oblige the countries that manage their fiscal and monetary affairs prudently to support those that mismanage their monetary affairs altogether; that oblige the "surplus" countries to support the "deficit" countries; that permit debtor countries to put off payment in gold indefinitely and compel other countries to become or remain their creditors. This means that the "special drawing rights"—"paper gold"—should never have been permitted to come into existence.

The "gold-exchange" standard (more accurately, the dollar-exchange standard) should be liquidated. This means that the United States should stand ready to redeem in gold on demand the present dollar-holdings of foreign central banks, and that these banks should by a self-denying agreement refuse to increase their present holdings of dollars as part of their official "reserves," and provide for at least the gradual liquidation of such holdings.

The United States Government should abandon all exchange controls, all attempts to forbid, restrict, or penalize foreign travel, or purchases of imports, or foreign investments. Certainly not least, the government should repeal its 36-year-old prohibition on the purchase, sale, or ownership of gold by its own citizens.

The United States should plan for eventual return to a full gold standard. This will now probably have to be by stages. What seems most likely at the moment of writing is that we shall soon find ourselves off even the token gold standard we are now on. We will be probably unable to set up a full gold standard except at a much higher dollar-price for gold than the present $35 an ounce.

But it is too early to specify all the conditions of such an eventual return to gold. All we can say now is, that as long as the world's money continues on a fiat paper basis, there will be monetary unreliability and unsettlement, if not monetary chaos.

4. Repeal all minimum wage laws. Repeal the Norris-

LaGuardia Act of 1932. Repeal or drastically modify the Wagner-Taft-Hartley Acts of 1935 and 1947. Stop compelling employers by law to continue negotiating with unions that are making unreasonable or exorbitant demands. Allow struck employers to try to continue their business peaceably with non-strikers or with replacements for strikers. Forbid all intimidatory mass picketing. Enforce existing common law or written statutes against intimidation, vandalism and violence. Reduce the Taft-Hartley Act to a simple prohibition of discrimination against either union or non-union workers. If the unions refuse to accept this two-sided prohibition, repeal the law entirely.

5. Let the government refrain from all "guidelines" for prices or wages, all controls of prices, wages, interest rates or rents, and all threats of such controls.

6. Stop the continuous increase in the national burden of Social Security, housing subsidies, farm subsidies, and the rest of the proliferating "antipoverty" programs.

Only three or four specific suggestions can be offered here:

Several eminent economists (notably Professors James Buchanan and Colin Campbell) have shown how Social Security could be converted from its present ambiguous but compulsory mixture of insurance and relief to a voluntary insurance program.

Federal grants to the States and localities to pay for relief and "antipoverty" programs should either be discontinued entirely or made only to the poorer half or even the poorest fifth of the States. The latter plan would take the political profit out of Federal grants-in-aid.

There should of course be no attempt to seize the earnings of those who work in order to provide "guaranteed incomes" to those who won't work.

The army of relief and other subsidy recipients will
continue to grow, and the solvency of the government
will become increasingly untenable, as long as part of
the population can vote to force the other part to support it. Such eminent nineteenth and early twentieth
century liberals as John Stuart Mill and A. V. Dicey
agreed that the franchise should be withheld from the
recipient of poor relief as long as he remains on relief.
If the fear of offending or the temptation to propitiate
such voters could be removed, there would be a star-
tling improvement in the quality of candidates for
office. The whole tone of our public life would be raised.

7. The graduated personal income tax should be
abandoned in favor of a strictly proportional income
tax. The argument against the "progressive" tax rate
was conclusively stated as long ago as 1833 by the Scot-
tish economist J. R. McCulloch: "The moment you abandon the cardinal principle of exacting from all
individuals *the same proportion of their income or of
their property,* you are at sea without rudder or com-
pass, and there is no amount of injustice and folly you
may not commit."

It is also clear that no income tax rate above 50 per
cent should be permitted. It is prima facie confiscation
when a man is allowed to keep less than half of his
earnings for his own family.

We have already seen that the income tax rates above
50 per cent raise negligible revenue, and that even with
present profligate spending a flat income tax rate of 21
per cent would raise all the revenue now being raised
from the whole range of rates from 14 to 77 per cent.

8. The present appalling power and omnipresence
of government must be forced back within tolerable
limits. Traditional liberals since Adam Smith have
agreed on only two indispensable functions of government: first, to protect the nation against aggression or

invasion from any other nation; and second, to protect every member of the community from the aggression, injustice, or oppression of any other member.

Some libertarians would add other functions: the provision of sewage, water, and other health and safety services in cities, the construction and maintenance of streets and roads, and, for national governments, the provision of a trustworthy monetary system, the setting of standards of weights and measures, and the collection and publication of certain kinds of information.

But about the nature and precise limits of these other governmental duties there is considerable disagreement. What can be said with confidence is that every extension of the functions and powers of the State beyond its primary duty of maintaining peace and justice should be scrutinized with jealous vigilance. Precisely because the State has the monopoly of coercion it can be allowed the monopoly *only* of coercion. Only if the modern State can be held within a strictly limited agenda of duties and powers can it be prevented from regimenting, conquering, and ultimately devouring the society which gave it birth.

The solution to our problems is not more paternalism, laws, decrees, and controls, but the restoration of liberty and free enterprise, the restoration of incentives, to let loose the tremendous constructive energies of 200 million Americans.

Index

Guaranteed incomes, 62-64, 65-
77, 78, 79, 80, 81, 82, 83,
84, 85, 86, 88, 89, 90, 91,
93, 95, 96, 97, 99, 100, 101,
104, 205, 218
Guaranteed jobs, 101-103, 104

Haberler, Professor Gottfried, 25
Hamilton, Alexander, 184
Health, Education, and Welfare,
Department of, 181, 201-202
Henry VIII, 51
Hoover Commission, 181
Housing and Urban Develop-
ment, Department of, 201
Hume, David, 12-13

IBM, 74
IMF. *See* International Monetary
Fund
Incentive, 77, 79, 81-82, 83, 84,
85, 86, 87, 88, 90, 91, 93,
95, 109, 135, 166, 198, 211,
220
Income tax: corporation, 109-114;
graduated, 104, 105-108,
189, 219; rates in foreign
countries, 105, 106, 107; revisions necessary, 219
Industrial Revolution, 64, 96
Inflation, 8-9, 13-14, 15, 17, 20,
32, 33, 34, 35, 40, 83, 130-
135, 136, 138-139, 143, 145,
146, 148-149, 150-152, 159,
161, 162-163, 166, 173, 178,
184, 212-213, 215, 216
Internal Revenue Service, 182
International Monetary Fund, 17,
19, 20, 21, 152, 158, 159,
160, 163, 200, 213, 216
International Monetary Statistics,
152
Interstate Commerce Commission, 182

Interstate Land Sales Full Disclosure Act of 1967, 49
Investment: corporate income tax
a discouragement to, 109,
110-112, 113-114; in foreign
countries, 176-177, 179, 217;
inflation a stimulus to, 134;
optimum conditions for, 135

Johnson, Lyndon B., 11, 18, 19,
33, 49, 50, 51, 52, 67, 172,
181, 192, 206, 210
Joint Economic Committee, Congressional, 63, 74
Jonson, Ben, 155

Kennedy, John F., 49, 51
Keynes, John Maynard, 5, 6-8,
130, 158
Kingsport strike, 203
Kohler strike, 203

Labor Standards Act of 1938, 24
Labor Statistics, Bureau of, 67
Labor unions, 25, 26, 27, 28, 32,
136, 187, 202, 218
Laissez faire, 185, 186
Land reform, 172, 173, 176
Larkin, Arthur E., Jr., 52
Lecky, W. E. H., 108
Libertarians, the task for, 199-
214, 216-220
Lindsay, John, 103
Locke, John, 47, 196
Louis XV, 191

McCulloch, J. R., 219
McGraw-Hill Book Company, 192
Machinery and Allied Products
Institute of Washington, 113
Man Versus The State, The 185,
186-192, 193, 195